CATHERINE REILLY was born in Stretford and educated at a convent grammar school in Manchester. She is a professional librarian and was Assistant Borough Librarian for Trafford from 1974–1980. Her first book, *English Poetry of the First World War: a bibliography* (1978), was the result of four years' research for a Fellowship of the Library Association. In 1980, Catherine Reilly was awarded a Major State Studentship to Merton College, Oxford, to do research into English poetry of the Second World War. Her home is in Chorlton-cum-Hardy, Manchester.

Scars Upon My Heart is the first anthology of women war poets of the First World War for over sixty years. The work of these eighty or so poets will come as a surprise to many. It shows, for example, that women were writing protest poetry before Wilfred Owen and Siegfried Sassoon, and that the view of 'the women at home', ignorant and idealistic, was quite false. Some of these poems come out of direct experience of nursing the victims of trench warfare; others record the pain of lovers, brothers, sons lost. Here, as elsewhere, the 'poetry is in the pity', and the anthology is a moving record of women's consciousness at a momentous period of history.

Virago

If you would like to know more about Virago books, write to us at Ely House, 37 Dover Street, London W1X 4HS for a full catalogue.

Please send a stamped addressed envelope

Scars Upon My Heart

**WOMEN'S POETRY AND VERSE OF THE
FIRST WORLD WAR**

Edited and introduced by
CATHERINE W. REILLY

With a preface by
JUDITH KAZANTZIS

Virago

Published by VIRAGO PRESS Limited 198
Ely House, 37 Dover Street, London W1X 4HS

Reprinted 1982

Typeset by King's English Typesetters Ltd, Cambridg
Printed in Finland by Werner Söderström Oy
a member of Finnprint

British Library Cataloguing in Publication Data

Scars upon my heart.
  1.English poetry – Woman authors
  2. English poetry – 20th century
  3. European War, 1914–1918 – Poetry
  I. Reilly, Catherine
  821′ .912′ 080358 PR1177
ISBN 0-86068-226-9

INDEXED IN GRANGERS

TO MY MOTHER

Your battle-wounds are scars upon my heart,
  Received when in that grand and tragic 'show'
You played your part
  Two years ago . . . .

✾ CONTENTS

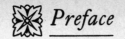

To read this book through from cover to cover is an extraordinary experience – and one I would suggest as a best first way to grasp the historical tragedy that lies behind these poems.

The voices of despair and endurance and anger are quiet, yet they mount steadily into a cumulative effect. Always behind them I am aware of the fraught gigantic backdrop of the War, the reality of 'The Shadow' of Rose Macaulay's poem. Against this looming 'Fear' and 'Pain' and 'Hell', where the young men are submerged, the woman's voice, as Catherine Reilly names it, becomes a tragic one, in several senses. From her uneasy position on the 'Rim of the shadow of the Hell' Rose Macaulay speaks sometimes with angry brilliance, sometimes with grateful idealism; there sounds under both a plain forlorn note.

We know of the male agony of the trenches from the poetry of soldiers like Sassoon and Owen. We know little in poetry of what that agony and its millions of deaths meant to the millions of English women who had to endure them – to learn to survive survival. This anthology fills a poignant gap. Just as the soldier poets with their personal experience of the fighting came to speak for a 'lost generation', so, much more modestly yet still truly, these women poets speak for the women whose own lives were often blighted by that miserable loss.

The war divided women and men not only by death: sad irony. Sweepingly Sassoon attacked women's romantic ignorance of its real nature in his piece 'Glory of Women': 'You love us when we're heroes, home on leave, / Or wounded in a mentionable place. . . .' The Jingo woman, answering Julian Grenfell, the warrior poet, may see the war partly as a holy rite, partly with maternal indulgence as a jolly game for the boys; but most poets here understand that war is no game, and they feel the insidious gulf between those who fought and those who waited – helpless to help the helpless.

So here is a part answer over many years to that soldiers' bitterness. As a representative voice it varies widely in poetic form, in skill and in argument. But horror of war pervades it.

After all, if women could not share the beastliness of the fighting – though many were in some sort of uniform by 1918, relatively few got near the front – they intimately shared its results: the wiping out of lovers, husbands, fathers, brothers and friends. The bereavements that touched enormous numbers of English women during those years have become a historical cliché. We have the stereotype of the bride who never was, who went on to make the emancipated career-woman of the twenties and thirties. Yet do we forget, in that well-known piece of social history, the individual roots of it? How fresh that tragedy becomes in these pages.

But first and foremost the poems mourn for the dead.

The note of grief is twofold: personal and general. Some poems simply relate the death of (or the anxiety for) the one loved. There is the delicate beauty of Katherine Tynan's 'A Girl's Song'; there is the bare account given in Eleanor Farjeon's 'Easter Monday'; or there is the wider perspective, yet still intensely personal nature, of 'Afterwards', Margaret Postgate Cole's bitter elegy (one of the best poems, as she is one of the best poets):

> And if these years have made you into a pit-prop,
> To carry the twisting galleries of the world's reconstruction
> (Where you may thank God, I suppose
> That they set you the sole stay of a nasty corner)
> What use is it to you? What use
> To have your body lying here
> In Sheer, underneath the larches?

Each of these various poems share the same stark cry: you were here, now you are dead. Meanwhile Charlotte Mew's poems, with their long marvellous alliterations, are imbued with suffering sympathy for bereaved women.

> To those who sit today with their great Dead, hands in their hands,
>   eyes in their eyes,
> At one with Love, at one with Grief: blind to the scattered things and
>   changing skies.

Some poems turn to the relative stranger, the Unknown Soldier. Here is the second kind of mourning: grief for the millions dead. Sometimes the elegy is spoken directly for all, as in Margaret

Postgate Cole's fine 'The Falling Leaves', a lament for the wholesale sacrifice of youth.

The centre is elegiac; but much else clusters around it. Authentic writing comes out of recording the home scene – the main option open to women writers. At home there is physical safety: despite Nancy Cunard's deadly serious description of 'Zeppelins', there is no continuous Blitz to endure. Yet the grind, along with the joking, is there: working-class poverty, middle-class war-shortages, officers' last leaves, wistful rural backwaters seen at all income-levels and tenderly described in the Georgian tradition; Jingoism rampant; London both grim and feckless; hospitals; soldiers wounded and unwounded; public schools; anxious mothers contemplating their small sons; varieties of war work, including the ubiquitous socks – all done from a middle-class viewpoint, despite the sallies into Kiplingesque Cockney.

Others get over something of the physical chaos of war itself. You sense it in May Sinclair's description of an army in retreat. Her testimony and that of other nurses or V.A.D.s is fascinating since they knew, if not the fighting, at least its immediate results – the extraordinary streams of casualties. At their best they supplement the descriptions of trench warfare by the male poets. Such 'service' poems feel active – part of the action. Some positively burst with praise for the 'grit' and 'pluck' of the men, marching or wounded or dying.

To plunge into the eye of war's hurricane – the fighting itself – required the use of strong imaginative devices. Some work, others not. The transferred voice is especially risky. To go 'Over the Top' as a Cockney private who reverts to God at the last with never a hint of an eff or a blind – this produces touching rather than good poetry. It is simply a measure of the yearning 'to be there', half romantic, half altruistic, an odd mixture – giving grounds for the use of that famous smear-word 'sentimental', which has been so generously applied down the critical ages to all parts of women's poetry.

Sentimentality and patriotism certainly went together during the Great War years. Nowadays, we have less time for Rupert Brooke and his solemn young heroism. We listen now to Sassoon and Owen – reluctant heroes both, though in the end they both stayed submissive to the high-minded macho ethic of the English officer. In the same way, some of the poetry here (and not only the Jingo jingles, but also some much finer) must read dated simply because it embraces confidently the patriotic, and religious, English cause.

Even Alice Meynell's 'Summer in England, 1914', which with handsome outrage draws the contrast between the beauty of the English countryside and the horror of the slaughter, submits to this twin ethic by the poem's end. She tells herself:

> Chide thou no more, O thou unsacrificed!
> The soldier dying dies upon a kiss,
> The very kiss of Christ.

The reluctant implication is: That very horror is necessary to protect that very beauty, that peace.

Unreservedly May Wedderburn Cannan in 'Rouen', with Masefield-like memory, expresses the patriotic excitement:

> Can you recall the parcels that we made them for the railroad,
> Crammed and bulging parcels held together by their string,
> And the voices of the sergeants who called the Drafts together,
> And the agony and splendour when they stood to save the King?

This is the poetry of England, inalienable from Honour, Duty, God, Christ and Sacrifice. This poetry sees as glorious not war itself but certainly the sacrifice of youth. And it accepts that purposeful Sacrifice with enormous gratitude. All flows from Duty. That duty is the world task of keeping alive English values; and then of guarding the sanctity of the English hearth and homeland against the militaristic enemy that threatens all this. If we don't remember the archaic glow of belief in the Imperial task, we lose the idealistic moving force behind 'Lamplight', also by May Wedderburn Cannan. If we don't remember that in 1914 middle-class England was a Christian country, we lose the numinous glow behind the word 'England'. In short, the orthodox Great War belief in the English cause against the Germans, and in the backing of an English God – and great gratitude to the protagonists of all this, the English fighting men – is of the essence in many of these poems. Helen Hamilton herself, that diagnostician of hypocrisy, spells out the received wisdom that the men are dying for the women. Thus – so the received wisdom goes on – the women themselves, the embodiment of Mother England at her most precious, shall live on to ensure the race in freedom and in peace.

The religious metaphor often takes over for the patriotic: the fighting men become Christ on Calvary (sacrificing themselves, and being sacrificed, for Love and Peace). Lucy Whitmell's 'Christ in Flanders' is full, over-full, of this idea. It vies with Madeline Ida Bedford's 'The Parson's Job' as the most sermonising poem in the book. (Both are of course preaching acceptance of the war to the working classes.) But Margaret Sackville's 'Sacrament' is quite a fine sensuous mystic example of the genre (widespread in those years).

Sometimes the poet, as Mary H. J. Henderson in 'An Incident', goes as far as identifying herself with Mary, Christ's mother, sharing humbly in the Sacrifice. Not too far into the book is Helen Hamilton's 'The Romancing Poet'. The two may be enjoyed together – one of the pleasurable pairings Catherine Reilly's wide net offers to the historian.

Christ, then, is crucified, and the duty of the woman, bereaved and despairing, becomes clear. She will live her life as the dead one bequeathed it to her. She will immortalise him in her obedience to the values for which he died. To question those values is to question the Sacrifice itself – impossible. For then his death must become not only horrible but also meaningless.

Therefore, as the death toll mounts, and bitterness grows in place of enthusiasm, it grows only against the enemy. This is the mood of Elinor Jenkins' 'Dulce Et Decorum?'. It is the personal mood of revenge which acquiesced in the grand 'slogging match' between the Powers of the later war years.

It is possibly easier to know that you yourself will probably be dying at random for nothing very much that you can see than to agree that your loved one has done so, with all the disloyalty that that implies. These were the respective hard truths that faced, and divided, men and women during the Great War. The stiff-upper-lip tradition cannot have helped – both sexes feeling they had to cheer each other on. 'We dare not weep who must be brave in battle,' writes Iris Tree. Did this sort of well-meant stoicism among women come over as callous to the men – the background perhaps to the hurt of Sassoon's lines?

And so I read many of the 'patriotic' poems with mixed emotion. They read to me not of superficiality or of hypocrisy, but more of a fearsome desperate nobility. It is the nobility of people who felt sucked into an inevitable tide. In this fated atmosphere even those who came to distrust the cause could be seduced by the excitement of war, as Vera Brittain brilliantly shows in her *Testament of Youth*.

And 'Love' – how often the word becomes a double shorthand for love of country and for personal love, both divinely elevated. The belief, the hope, may be simple: that Love must conquer Death in the end. Iris Tree's impressive 'Of all who died in silence far away' ends on this thought. Yet here is a poem which shifts away from comfortable patriotism. She evokes the soldier rather more as a tortured, deserted Christ.

Less abstractly, others trust in love, feeling more personally that the loved one cannot die, that he lives on within the woman's heart, and that a personal bargain of remembrance will keep him always somehow alive; or that in the end, somehow, living or dying, all are one. Such a stratagem of hope may come from one who believed in the rightfulness of the Sacrifice, or on the contrary from those who thought it doubtful: it's a way of surviving survival that crosses formal belief. And here I come properly to the other response to the war: protest.

And here also I must raise with bewilderment the near-as-maybe non-presence of women in modern Great War anthologies. For Catherine Reilly has retrieved intelligent and vigorous poetry and verse of scorn and denunciation, well in line with modern dislike of Great War heroics. These poems, whether light or grimly satirical, are the mirror images of some of those mentioned above. Lesbia Thanet's small personal statement makes a starting-place. Elizabeth Chandler Forman's deceptively gentle ballad sends up war nationalism absolutely.

God is dead, say others, war is not only horrible but perhaps futile; certainly run on hypocrisy. The young soldiers are the brave, pathetic dupes of war glory: the war glory that Ruth Comfort Mitchell attacks so resoundingly and rollickingly:

> They are braggart attitudes we've worn so long;
> They are tinsel platitudes we've sworn so long –

Emily Orr's recruit from the slums is the bottom of the heap, and cannon-fodder for Mother England. And in May Herschel-Clarke's ' "For Valour" ' the working-class woman is the bottom of the civilian heap. (But she's a pleasant get-back to Madeline Ida Bedford's persuasive parson.) Civilians, men and women too, are 'Ghouls' or white-feather bullies (Helen Hamilton); or carrion-flies, in Edith Sitwell's powerful image of war fatigue and war hysteria.

> We are the dull blind carrion-fly
> That dance and batten. Though God die
> Mad from the horror of the light –
> The light is mad, too, flecked with blood, –
> We dance, we dance, each night.

Peace itself becomes a doubtful quantity. And for some – in Elizabeth Daryush's grand 'For a Survivor of the Mesopotamian Campaign' – it will never be possible again. As for the demobilised, says Vera Brittain with drawled irony, they are for the scrapheap. Going back to the war, Winifred M. Letts describes that lowest of the low, 'The Deserter'. Margery Lawrence, in 'Transport of Wounded in Mesopotamia, 1917', roundly identifies with the soldiers against the civilians in an angrily effective cross-over very different from her simple patriotic lament of a year before.

Given this angry identification with the victim soldiers there is little straight evidence for that feminist protest that repudiates war as the outcome of compulsive male aggressiveness or, anyway, of the patriarchal mode. In fact Catherine Reilly points out how some feminism runs the other way – a wish to be with the men.

Still, S. Gertrude Ford assumes that women left to themselves would not have chosen the war. Interestingly, the one piece ('Women at Munition Making' by Mary Gabrielle Collins) that defines war as a male abomination proceeds from the heart of angel-on-the-hearth anti-feminism. As for the historic emancipation of millions of women out of domestic service into munitions and other factory work, it is the jingoistic Jessie Pope who approves – as long as they quit when the men get home.

But 'Ghouls', with its young men supported against the old, does have an anti-patriarchal ring about it. Meanwhile Gabrielle Elliot's 'Pierrot Goes to War' gently chides macho war romance from deserted Pierrette's point of view. Pauline Barrington may be the first poet in the language to plead against war toys for boys. Mary Webb's bejewelled Tennysonian lament has soldiers playing at the war game generation by generation.

'O children, come in from your soldier-play
In the black bean tents! The night is falling. . . .'

But anti-macho criticism is inherent in many of the anti-war pieces mentioned above.

Protest, and naïve patriotism, and many thoughtful stirrings in between. Yet unity exists, despite the divisions in this 'women's voice'. It exists not only in the grief, but also in the admiration for the man. If one or two doubt his better sense, all agree on his courage. Though the word 'sacrifice' takes on wry overtones in some mouths, all agree that one way or another a sacrifice has been made, glorious, terrible or monstrous, and that it must not be forgotten, nor the men themselves. Ursula Roberts' contempt for the Remembrance ceremony in 'The Cenotaph' is diametrically opposed to Charlotte Mew's 'The Cenotaph 1919'. Yet both are talking about remembrance. Ironically, and from different points of view, this old theme, 'lest we forget', unites all.

I hope that this anthology, like Vera Brittain's autobiography reissued, will make flesh some of the griefs, certainties, doubts and despairs of the English women who lived through the Great War, and that it will redeem them from the clutches of the 'white feather' image. And I wonder, after all, if the invisibility to date of women's poetry on the Great War doesn't stem from something quite deep in the patriarchal mind – the folk memory that nurses that 'white feather' image along – the same which generates a general lack of interest in women's wartime experience, including the endlessly repeated tragic one of bereavement.

The particular furious magnificence of the soldier poets makes it unsurprising that women poets should recede into the background. Yet to be so little known now?

Is there among men, not excluding editors of war-poetry anthologies, the atavistic feeling that war is man's concern, as birth is woman's; and that women quite simply cannot speak on the matter – an illogic which holds sway even when women have done so with knowledge and talent? It would be an understandable illogic. For men in the Great War had to die and women did not; and, moreover, men died in their millions, according to the official and explicit credo, for Mother England – that their women should live, protected, in peace. Deep emotions might well fuel such an illogic, handed down over the decades by patriarchal tradition – that women had nothing to say on the war.

Whether such a deep system has operated, who knows? It is of course nonsense that women have nothing to do with war. Even in the Great War with its huge partitions of the sexes, it was a nonsense: and I do not simply refer to women's war work.

Yet, just as men often feel they have a bit part during childbirth, so women during war-time. I have suggested that many of these poems are about ways to survive survival. They are equally about ways to find a role. Not an easy position, on the 'Rim of the shadow of the Hell'. It led to some loud posturing; it certainly led to many more acts of heart-rending stoical support.

In the end Sassoon's 'Glory of Women' is unfair because it presented women with a catch. If they encouraged their men, they were heartless; but how if (as some courageously did, of course) they had backed out, refused to be brave, opposed the man's own grim determination to act creditably in what was after all a male-run 'show'?

Empathy between the sexes had to operate over the divide of

land and sea, and over a dividing wasteland of experience. Many of these poems reach into that wasteland painfully. Some cross it with triumph.

Judith Kazantzis, London 1981

✤ *Acknowledgements*

I am most grateful to all those who have helped me, in various ways, to complete this work. In particular I thank Alan Young and Michael Redhead, who were the first to view my selection with a critical eye; Victor Schwarz, who 'found' the title; H. J. D. Cole, Stephen Dobell, Gordon Phillips (Archivist, Times Newspapers Ltd), Charles Seaton (Librarian, *Spectator*) and Mrs E. A. Stapleforth, all of whom went to some trouble to assist with certain biographical notes on the poets.

Permission to reprint copyright poems in this book is gratefully acknowledged. Apologies are offered to those copyright-holders whom it has proved impossible to locate.

Marian Allen: 'The Raiders' and 'The Wind on the Downs' from *The Wind on the Downs*, published 1918 by Humphreys.

Lilian M. Anderson: 'Leave in 1917' from *Contemporary Devonshire and Cornwall Poetry*, edited by S. Fowler Wright, published 1930 by S. Fowler Wright.

Pauline Barrington: ' "Education" ' from *Poems Written during the Great War 1914–1918*, edited by Bertram Lloyd, published 1918 by George Allen & Unwin Ltd. Reprinted by permission of George Allen & Unwin Ltd.

Madeline Ida Bedford: 'Munition Wages' and 'The Parson's Job' from *The Young Captain*, published 1917 by Erskine Macdonald Ltd.

Maud Anna Bell: 'From a Trench' from *A Treasury of War Poetry*, edited by G. H. Clarke, published 1919 by Hodder & Stoughton Ltd. Reprinted by permission of *The Times*.

Nora Bomford: 'Drafts' from *Poems of a Pantheist*, published 1918 by Chatto & Windus Ltd.

Sybil Bristowe: 'Over the Top' from *The Lyceum Book of War Verse*, edited by A. E. Macklin, published 1918 by Erskine Macdonald Ltd.

Vera Brittain: 'The Lament of the Demobilised' from *Oxford Poetry 1920*, published 1920 by B. H. Blackwell, Oxford. 'Perhaps—' and 'To My Brother' from *Verses of a V.A.D.*, published 1918 by Erskine Macdonald Ltd. Reprinted by permission of Mr Paul Berry, Literary Executor of the Estate of the late Vera Brittain.

May Wedderburn Cannan: 'Lamplight', 'Rouen', 'Since They Have Died' and 'Love, 1916' from *In War Time*, published 1917 by B. H. Blackwell, Oxford. Reprinted by permission of Mr James C. Slater.

Isabel Constance Clarke: 'Anniversary of the Great Retreat' from *The Pathway of Dreams*, published 1919 by Sands & Co. Ltd.

Margaret Postgate Cole: 'The Falling Leaves' and 'Afterwards' from *Poems*, published 1918 by George Allen & Unwin Ltd. 'Praematuri' and 'The Veteran' from *An Anthology of War Poems*, edited by Frederick Brereton, published 1930 by William Collins & Co. Ltd. Reprinted by permission of Mr H. J. D. Cole.

Mary Gabrielle Collins: 'Women at Munition Making' from *Branches unto the Sea*, published 1916 by Erskine Macdonald Ltd.

Alice Corbin: 'Fallen' from *Poems of the Great War*, edited by J. W. Cunliffe, published 1916 by The Macmillan Company, New York. Reprinted by Books for Libraries Press. Distributed by Arno Press, Inc.

Nancy Cunard: 'Zeppelins' from *Outlaws*, published 1921 by Elkin Mathews. Reprinted by permission of Mr A. R. A. Hobson on behalf of The Estate of the late Nancy Cunard.

Elizabeth Daryush: 'Flanders Fields' and 'Unknown Warrior' from *Verses*, published 1930 by Oxford University Press. 'For a Survivor of the Mesopotamian Campaign' from *Verses: Third Book*, published 1933 by Oxford University Press. 'Subalterns' from *Verses: Fourth Book*, published 1934 by Oxford University Press. Reprinted by permission of Mr A. A. Daryush.

Helen Dircks: 'After Bourlon Wood' and 'London in War' from *Passenger*, published 1920 by Chatto & Windus Ltd. Reprinted by permission of the author and Chatto & Windus.

Eva Dobell: 'Pluck', 'Gramophone Tunes' and 'Night Duty' from *A Bunch of Cotswold Grasses*, published 1919 by Arthur H. Stockwell Ltd. Reprinted by permission of Mr P. H. M. Dobell.

Helen Parry Eden: 'A Volunteer' from *Coal and Candlelight*, published 1918 by The Bodley Head.

Gabrielle Elliot: 'Pierrot Goes to War' from *A Treasury of War Poetry, 2nd Series*, edited by G. H. Clarke, published 1919 by Houghton Mifflin Company, New York. Reprinted by permission of The New York Times Company.

Eleanor Farjeon: 'Easter Monday' from *First and Second Love*, published 1959 by Oxford University Press. 'Peace' and 'Now That You Too' from *Sonnets and Poems*, published 1918 by B. H. Blackwell, Oxford. Reprinted by permission of David Higham Associates Ltd.

S. Gertrude Ford: ' "A Fight to a Finish" ' and 'Nature in War-Time' from *A Fight to a Finish*, published 1917 by C. W. Daniel & Co. Ltd. 'The Tenth Armistice Day' from *The England of My Dream*, published 1928 by C. W. Daniel & Co. Ltd.

Elizabeth Chandler Forman: 'The Three Lads' from *War Verse*, edited by Frank Foxcroft, published 1919 by The Thomas Y. Crowell Company, New York. Reprinted by permission of The Thomas Y. Crowell Company, New York.

Lillian Gard: 'Her "Allowance"!' from *The Country Life Anthology of Verse*, edited by Peter A. Graham, published 1915 by *Country Life* and Newnes. Reprinted by permission of The Hamlyn Publishing Group Ltd.

Muriel Elsie Graham: 'The Lark above the Trenches' and 'The Battle of the Swamps' from *Collected Poems*, published 1930 by Williams & Norgate Ltd. Reprinted by permission of Ernest Benn Ltd.

Nora Griffiths: 'The Wykhamist' from *The Country Life Anthology of Verse*, edited by Peter A. Graham, published 1915 by *Country Life* and Newnes. Reprinted by permission of The Hamlyn Publishing Group Ltd.

Diana Gurney: 'The Fallen' from *Verses*, published 1926 by Cayme Press.

Cicely Hamilton: 'Non-Combatant' from *Poems of the Great War*, edited by J. W. Cunliffe, published 1916 by The Macmillan Company, New York. Reprinted by Books for Libraries Press. Distributed by Arno Press, Inc.

Helen Hamilton: 'The Ghouls', 'The Jingo-Woman' and 'The Romancing Poet' from *Napoo!*, published 1918 by B. H. Blackwell, Oxford.

Ada May Harrison: 'New Year, 1916' from *Cambridge Poets, 1914–1920*, edited by Edward Davison, published 1920 by Heffer, Cambridge.

Mary H. J. Henderson: 'An Incident' from *The Lyceum Book of War Verse*, edited by Alys Eyre Macklin, published 1918 by Erskine Macdonald Ltd.

Agnes Grozier Herbertson: 'Airman, R.F.C.' from *This Is the Hour*, published 1942 by Fortune Press. Reprinted by permission of Charles Skilton Ltd. 'The Seed-Merchant's Son' from *The Quiet Heart*, published 1919 by Elkin Mathews.

May Herschel-Clarke: ' "For Valour" ' and ' "Nothing to Report" ' from *Behind the Firing Line*, published ,1917 by Erskine Macdonald Ltd.

Teresa Hooley: 'A War Film' from *Songs of All Seasons*, published 1927 by Jonathan Cape Ltd. Reprinted by permission of The Estate of the late Teresa Hooley, and Jonathan Cape Ltd.

Elinor Jenkins: 'Dulce Et Decorum?' from *Poems; Last Poems*, published 1921 by Sidgwick & Jackson Ltd. Reprinted by permission of Sidgwick & Jackson Ltd.

Anna Gordon Keown: 'Reported Missing' from *War Verse*, edited by Frank Foxcroft, published 1919 by The Thomas Y. Crowell Company, New York. Reprinted by permission of The Thomas Y. Crowell Company, New York.

Margery Lawrence: 'The Lost Army' and 'Transport of Wounded in Mesopotamia, 1917' from *Fourteen to Forty-Eight*, published 1949 by Robert Hale Ltd. Reprinted by permission of The Estate of the late Margery Lawrence, and Laurence Pollinger Ltd.

Winifred M. Letts: 'Casualty', 'Screens' and 'What Reward?' from *The Spires of Oxford*, published 1917 by E. P. Dutton, New York. 'The Deserter' from *Hallowe'en and Poems of the War*, published 1916 by Smith, Elder & Co. Reprinted by permission of John Murray (Publishers) Ltd.

Olive E. Lindsay: 'Despair' from *A Little Rhyme*, published 1925 by Oliver & Boyd, Edinburgh.

Amy Lowell: 'Convalescence' from *The Complete Poetical Works of Amy Lowell*, published 1955 by Houghton Mifflin Company. Reprinted by permission of Houghton Mifflin Company.

Rose Macaulay: 'Picnic' and 'The Shadow' from *Three Days*, published 1919 by Constable & Co. Ltd. Reprinted by permission of A. D. Peters & Co. Ltd.

Nina Macdonald: 'Sing a Song of War-Time' from *War-Time Nursery Rhymes*, published 1918 by Routledge & Kegan Paul Ltd. Reprinted by permission of Routledge & Kegan Paul Ltd.

Florence Ripley Mastin: 'At the Movies' from *A Treasury of War Poetry, 2nd Series*, edited by G. H. Clarke, published 1919 by Houghton Mifflin Company. Reprinted by permission of The New York Times Company.

Charlotte Mew: 'The Cenotaph', 'May, 1915' and 'June, 1915' from *Collected Poems*, published 1953 by Gerald Duckworth & Co. Ltd. Reprinted by permission of Gerald Duckworth & Co. Ltd.

Alice Meynell: 'Lord, I Owe Thee a Death' and 'Summer in England, 1914' from *Poems. Complete Edition*, published 1940 by Burns, Oates & Washbourne Ltd.

Ruth Comfort Mitchell: 'He Went for a Soldier' from *Poems of the Great War*, edited by J. W. Cunliffe, published 1916 by The Macmillan Company, New York. Reprinted by Books for Libraries Press. Distributed by Arno Press, Inc.

Harriet Monroe: 'On the Porch' from *Poems of the Great War*, edited by J. W. Cunliffe, published 1916 by The Macmillan Company, New York. Reprinted by Books for Libraries Press. Distributed by Arno Press, Inc.

Edith Nesbit: 'The Fields of Flanders' and 'Spring in War-Time' from *Many Voices*, published 1922 by Hutchinson & Co. Ltd.

Eileen Newton: 'Last Leave' and 'Revision' from *Lamps in the Valley*, published 1927 by Elkin Mathews & Marrot.

Eleanour Norton: 'In a Restaurant, 1917' from *Magic,*

published 1922 by Wilson, London.

Carola Oman: 'Ambulance Train 30' and 'Brussels, 1919' from *The Menin Road*, published 1919 by Hodder & Stoughton Ltd. Reprinted by permission of Mr P. R. O. Stuart.

May O'Rourke: 'The Minority: 1917' from *West Wind Days*, published 1918 by Erskine Macdonald Ltd.

Emily Orr: 'A Recruit from the Slums' from *A Harvester of Dreams*, published 1922 by Burns, Oates & Washbourne Ltd.

Jessie Pope: 'The Call' and 'Socks' from *War Poems*, published 1915 by Grant Richards. 'The Nut's Birthday' from *More War Poems*, published 1915 by Grant Richards. 'War Girls' from *Simple Rhymes for Stirring Times*, published 1916 by C. Arthur Pearson. Reprinted by permission of The Hamlyn Publishing Group Ltd.

Inez Quilter: ' "Sall" ' from *A Book of Poems for the Blue Cross Fund*, published 1917 by Jarrolds Publishers (London) Ltd.

Dorothy Una Ratcliffe: 'Remembrance Day in the Dales' from *Singing Rivers*, published 1922 by The Bodley Head. Reprinted by permission of Mrs Ludi Horenstein.

Ursula Roberts ('Susan Miles'): 'The Cenotaph' from *Annotations* by 'Susan Miles', published 1922 by Oxford University Press. Reprinted by permission of Oxford University Press.

Margaret Sackville: 'A Memory' from *The Pageant of War*, published 1916 by Simpkin, Marshall, Hamilton, Kent & Co. Ltd. 'Sacrament' from *Collected Poems*, published 1939 by Martin Secker.

Aimee Byng Scott: 'July 1st, 1916' from *The Road to Calais*, published 1919 by Thacker.

May Sinclair: 'Field Ambulance in Retreat' from *King Albert's Book*, edited by Hall Caine, published 1914 by Hodder & Stoughton Ltd. Reprinted by permission of Curtis Brown Ltd.

Edith Sitwell: 'The Dancers' from *Clowns' Houses*, published 1918 by B. H. Blackwell, Oxford. Reprinted by permission of David Higham Associates on behalf of the Estate of the late Dame Edith Sitwell.

Cicily Fox Smith: 'The Convalescent' from *Fighting Men*, published 1916 by Elkin Mathews.

Marie Carmichael Stopes: 'Night on the Shore' from *The Lyceum Book of War Verse*, edited by Alys Eyre Macklin, published 1918 by Erskine Macdonald Ltd.

Muriel Stuart: 'Forgotten Dead, I Salute You' from *Poems*, published 1922 by William Heinemann Ltd. Reprinted by permission of Mrs E. A. Stapleforth.

Millicent Sutherland: 'One Night' from *Lest We Forget*, edited by H. B. Elliott, published 1915 by Jarrolds Publishers (London) Ltd. Reprinted by permission of Elizabeth, Countess of Sutherland.

C.A.L.T.: 'Y.M.C.A.' from *A Pocketful of Rye*, privately printed [1916?] by Martin & Sturt, Farnham.

Sara Teasdale: 'Spring in War-Time' from *Poems of the Great War*, edited by J. W. Cunliffe, published 1916 by The Macmillan Company, New York. Reprinted by Books for Libraries Press. Distributed by Arno Press, Inc. ' "There Will Come Soft Rains" ' from *Collected Poems of Sara Teasdale*, copyright 1920 by Macmillan Publishing Co. Inc., New York, renewed 1948 by Mamie T. Wheless. Reprinted by permission of Macmillan Publishing Co. Inc., New York.

Lesbia Thanet: 'In Time of War' from *War Verse*, edited by Frank Foxcroft, published 1919 by The Thomas Y. Crowell Company, New York. Reprinted by permission of The Thomas Y. Crowell Company, New York.

Aelfrida Tillyard: 'Invitation au Festin' and 'A Letter from Ealing Broadway Station' from *The Garden and the Fire*, published 1916 by Heffer, Cambridge.

Iris Tree: 'Of all who died in silence far away . . .' and 'And afterwards, when honour has made good . . .' from *Poems*, published 1920 by The Bodley Head.

Alys Fane Trotter: 'The Hospital Visitor' from *Houses and Dreams*, published 1924 by B. H. Blackwell, Oxford.

Katharine Tynan: 'The Broken Soldier' from *Collected Poems*, published 1930 by Macmillan & Co. Ltd. 'A Girl's Song' and 'Joining the Colours' from *Flower of Youth*, published 1918 by Sidgwick & Jackson Ltd. Reprinted by permission of The Society of Authors and Miss Pamela Hinkson.

Viviane Verne: 'Kensington Gardens' from *A Casket of Thoughts*, published 1916 by Simpkin, Marshall, Hamilton, Kent & Co. Ltd.

Alberta Vickridge: 'In a V.A.D. Pantry' from *The Sea Gazer*, published 1919 by Erskine Macdonald Ltd.

Mary Webb: 'Autumn, 1914' from *Fifty-One Poems*, published 1946 by Jonathan Cape Ltd. Reprinted by permission of The Executors of the Mary Webb Estate.

M. Winifred Wedgwood: 'The V.A.D. Scullery-Maid's Song' and 'Christmas, 1916' from *Verses of a V.A.D. Kitchen-Maid*, published 1917 by Gregory & Scott Ltd, Torquay.

Catherine Durning Whetham: 'The Poet and the Butcher' from *An Exeter Book of Verse*, published 1919 by Eland, Exeter.

Lucy Whitmell: 'Christ in Flanders' from *An Anthology of War Poems*, edited by Frederick Brereton, published 1930 by William Collins & Co. Ltd.

Margaret Adelaide Wilson: 'Gervais' from *A Treasury of War Poetry*, edited by G. H. Clarke, published 1919 by Hodder & Stoughton Ltd.

Marjorie Wilson: 'To Tony (Aged 3)' from *A Treasury of War Poetry, 2nd Series*, edited by G. H. Clarke, published 1919 by Houghton Mifflin Company, New York.

Introduction

The vast quantity of poetry and verse published during the First World War, 1914–18, is now regarded as a phenomenon in the history of English literature. In fact, a popular enthusiasm for writing verse was evident from the turn of the century, reputedly prompting Ezra Pound to remark in 1910: 'Everybody's Aunt Lucy or Uncle George has written something-or-other.'[1] The private publication of a slim volume of verse was an indulgence practised widely by those who could afford to pay for it. Persons of more modest means could engage a local jobbing printer to reproduce their verse in pamphlet or broadsheet form, selling at perhaps one or two pence a copy.

So poetry was written, and presumably read, on quite a large scale. The newspapers and journals of the period are filled with verse – good, bad and indifferent. Whatever the poetic standard, the verse is redolent with the flavour of the time, and reflects popular opinion and the accepted standards. In 1914 the printed word was the prime means of mass communication in an era without radio and television broadcasting, although the silent cinema had been introduced some years before.

My own recent bibliographical research attempted to quantify the poetry of the First World War which had been published in book, pamphlet or broadsheet form.[2] It succeeded in identifying no fewer than 2225 British individuals, men and women, servicemen and civilians, who had written verse on the theme of this most terrible war. Of these 2225 at least 532 were women and at least 417 (men and women) served in the armed forces or other uniformed organisations such as the Red Cross, the Special Constabulary, and the Voluntary Aid Detachment.

The First World War was a gross folly and an immense agony for many nations. To the generations born after 1918 the obscenity of the war is epitomised in the privation and suffering borne by the men serving in the trenches of France and Flanders. The concept of whole armies fighting day after day, month after month for four long years, forced to exist in holes dug in unstable

[1] C. K. Stead, *The New Poetic* (Hutchinson, 1964), p. 53.
[2] Catherine W. Reilly, *English Poetry of the First World War: a Bibliography* (George Prior, 1978).

marshy terrain, winning then losing some few yards of ground at
the expense of enormous casualties, is clearly a tragic absurdity.
Naturally enough, the anthologies of Great War poetry pub-
lished in recent years tend to concentrate on the work of the
soldier poets who served on the Western Front. (As somebody
wryly remarked, it seemed as though every few yards of trench
sported its own poet, feverishly putting pen to paper between
bombardments.) These anthologies usually include some naval
and air force verse, and the work of such well-established literary
lions as Thomas Hardy, Rudyard Kipling, D. H. Lawrence and
W. B. Yeats. The contribution by women has been largely
ignored, although Philip Larkin includes May Wedderburn
Cannan's 'Rouen' in his choice for *The Oxford Book of Twentieth
Century English Verse*.[3] Only three other women – Charlotte
Mew, Alice Meynell and Fredegond Shove – are represented in
modern anthologies of First World War poetry.

This present collection is the result of curiosity as to why the
work of most of the 532 women poets traced in my bibliographical
study should have apparently faded into oblivion. Certainly some
very bad poems by women came to light, but so also did some very
bad poems by men. Although there was time only for the most
cursory check, it seemed that a positive 'women's voice' emerged
strongly. The introduction of Women's Studies into the academic
curriculum of many universities and colleges makes it impera-
tive that all feminine viewpoints be explored. In my desire to
make such poems available once again, I returned to the slim
volumes and the anthologies, searching for a representative
collection.

There are 125 poems in this anthology, the work of some 79
poets, one of whom is identified only by initials. Many of these
79 women were or became well known in various spheres –
predominantly, as one might expect, in the world of literature
and journalism. In contrast, some were so obscure it has been
impossible to trace any biographical details about them. Many of
the poems were written after the war, undoubtedly giving a
retrospective view of it, but what emerges with some clarity is

[3] Oxford University Press, 1973.

evidence that the received view of 'women at home' as ignorant and idealistic is quite false. Women were writing their own protest poetry long before Owen and Sassoon. Examples of this are Mary Gabrielle Collins' 'Women at Munition Making', S. Gertrude Ford's '"A Fight to a Finish"', May Herschel-Clarke's '"Nothing to Report"' and Winifred M. Letts' 'Screens' and 'What Reward?'.

Before military conscription for men became law in May 1916, some women helped organise mass recruitment meetings urging men to join the colours. That women handed white feathers to men not in uniform is undoubtedly true. These women seemed to regard this activity as legitimate war work. 'White feather' verse appeared regularly in newspapers and periodicals. Jessie Pope's 'The Call' is a comparatively mild example of the genre. Yet the 'white feather' women were strongly attacked in verse such as Helen Hamilton's 'The Jingo-Woman'.

Many women lamented the fact that they themselves were unable to play an active part in the fighting. Rose Macaulay was much vilified for the seemingly naïve sentiments expressed in her 'Many Sisters to Many Brothers' written in 1915:

> Oh it's you that have the luck, out there in blood and muck:
>   You were born beneath a kindly star;
> All we dreamt, I and you, you can really go and do,
>   And I can't, the way things are.
> In a trench you are sitting, while I am knitting
>   A hopeless sock that never gets done.
> Well, here's luck, my dear — and you've got it, no fear;
>   But for me . . . a war is poor fun.

This could not have been written after 1915, for the following year the appalling casualty-lists resulting from the battles on the Somme made people at home only too well aware of the grim reality and the grand scale of the slaughter. Included here are two other poems by Rose Macaulay, 'Picnic, July 1917' and 'The Shadow', both written in 1917, which give an entirely different perspective, removing the cliché view of the 'thoughts of women'. Nora Bomford, a pantheist, takes a small step towards feminism in 'Drafts', written towards the end of the war:

> O, damn the shibboleth
> Of sex! God knows we've equal personality.
> Why should men face the dark while women stay
> To live and laugh and meet the sun each day.

There are many other aspects of previously underestimated women's poetry which warrant investigation.

The poetry and verse in this collection will come as a surprise to many readers. Apart from significant social comment on this period of twentieth-century history, a strong sense of war's realities is expressed. There is a genuine rejection of false sentiment and false idealism, there is sympathy, compassion and honest responses of indignation and pity from women, some of whom had seen a little of the 'real thing' and were deeply moved by it.

Catherine W. Reilly, Manchester, 1981

THE RAIDERS

In shadowy formation up they rise,
Dusky raiders with their bat-like wings.
The night is studded with a thousand eyes
And its dim cloak on desolation flings.
The wind through stay and wire moans and whines,
The engines throb with thrilled expectant breath.
Eighty miles to eastward of the lines
They go and carry with them stings of death.
The spirit of Adventure calls ahead,
They leave the earth behind them battle-bound
And rise untrammelled from the war-stained ground,
Grey moving shadows o'er the lonely dead,
Flying unflinching as an arrow flies
Down the uncharted roadway of the skies.

THE WIND ON THE DOWNS

I like to think of you as brown and tall,
As strong and living as you used to be,
In khaki tunic, Sam Brown belt and all,
And standing there and laughing down at me.
Because they tell me, dear, that you are dead,
Because I can no longer see your face,
You have not died, it is not true, instead
You seek adventure in some other place.
That you are round about me, I believe;
I hear you laughing as you used to do,
Yet loving all the things I think of you;
And knowing you are happy, should I grieve?
You follow and are watchful where I go;
How should you leave me, having loved me so?

We walked along the tow-path, you and I,
Beside the sluggish-moving, still canal;
It seemed impossible that you should die;

1

I think of you the same and always shall.
We thought of many things and spoke of few,
And life lay all uncertainly before,
And now I walk alone and think of you,
And wonder what new kingdoms you explore.
Over the railway line, across the grass,
While up above the golden wings are spread,
Flying, ever flying overhead,
Here still I see your khaki figure pass,
And when I leave the meadow, almost wait
That you should open first the wooden gate.

Lilian M. Anderson

LEAVE IN 1917

Moonlight and death were on the Narrow Seas,
moonlight and death and sleep were on the land:
blindfold the lamps of home, but blinding bright
the wheeling, watching, searching lamps of war.
           To the lone pilot, homing like a dove,
his England was no England. Thought he not
of night-hushed fields and elms, of sleeping farms
where bats, like swallows, hawked about the eaves,
and the white moonlight still as water lay
upon the farmyard and the shippen roofs.
Thought he of hidden forts and hidden camps,
of furnaces down-slaked to darkness, towns
crouched slumbering beneath the threat of death.

North-west he held till, stooping, he could read
the map-small town of Bedford. Up and on.
Northampton fell behind him. Twenty miles,
and Avon lay, a winding thread of steel,
among its wraith-white meadows.
                     Low and lower
swept the still wings. Beyond the many roofs,
beyond the chimney-shafts, behind the hills,
the moon hung pallid in an empty sky.
Ached in his throat the scent of morning frost.
The wren-shrill song of every harping wire
was joyful in the silence. Coventry
was yet asleep, but out among the sheds,
new-lit on frosty grass, he found a welcome.

The crystalled dawn grew red, and the sun crept
above the sharp-rimmed hills. And Sheringham,
seeing the rays smoke white athwart the field,
knew that from dawn to dawn, and once again
from dawn to eve, pain-precious every hour,
lay – God be thanked for it! – two days of leave.

        . . . He travelled south and west.
And still to him his England was no England;

Until at last

but, rocking to the motion of the train,
half-sleeping where he stood, and sleeping quite
whenever chance and crowds and courtesy
would give him leave to rest, he dreamt of war,
of flights and stunts and crashes; tattered dreams
of month-old happenings.

                                        Until at last
his drowsiness was stirred by Devon names –
Exeter, Axminster,
Starcross and Dawlish Warren –
and from his dreams he woke to level waves
that broke on tide-wet shallows.

        Here was his England, stripped of mail and weapons,
child-sweet and maiden-gentle. Here was Spring,
her feet frost-bright among the daffodils.

                                Four months ago
when ice hung from the ferns beside the spring
and robins came for crumbs, had Sheringham,
new-wedded, brought his wife to Devonshire.
The little house stood half-way up the hill,
with milk-white walls, and slated paths that went
like stepping-stones, from April to October,
among a foam of flowers. Apple-trees
leaned from the orchard-slopes; the hillside grass
showed apple-green beneath. Four months ago
had ice hung from the ferns beside the spring:
now, as he climbed the hillside, Sheringham
saw snowdrops in the grass, and heard the lambs
in the Prior's Acre and the valley fields
calling and calling. Clear dripped the spring
beside the orchard-gate.

                        And 'God!' he prayed,
for sunset lay along the upper boughs
of every twisted tree, and emerald dusk
lay stirlessly beneath. And, still as dusk
because she feared to meet her happiness,
his wife stood waiting on the orchard-steps.

Love came to them, poor Love, with pinions torn –
poor Love, young Love, that should be auriole-winged.
Scarcely they dared to hold each other close,
young husband and young wife, scarcely to kiss,
lest they should shatter, by their very love,
this rainbow-fragile joy. For every kiss,
however sweet with joy, held lees of tears.
Like bees that garner sunshine-golden honey
against the barren winter, Sheringham
garnered his memories against the morrow.
Here was the slated threshold of his home,
and here his lighted hearth; here daffodils
shone amber in the firelight; here the breath
of violets and rosy hyacinths
clung heavy to the blue and bitter incense
of lately-kindled logs. And sweet, sweet, sweet
the finches singing in the orchard dusk!

Pauline Barrington

'EDUCATION'

The rain is slipping, dripping down the street;
The day is grey as ashes on the hearth.
The children play with soldiers made of tin,
        While you sew
        Row after row.

The tears are slipping, dripping one by one;
Your son has shot and wounded his small brother.
The mimic battle's ended with a sob,
        While you dream
        Over your seam.

The blood is slipping, dripping drop by drop;
The men are dying in the trenches' mud.
The bullets search the quick among the dead.
        While you drift,
        The Gods sift.

The ink is slipping, dripping from the pens,
On papers, White and Orange, Red and Grey, –
History for the children of tomorrow, –
        While you prate
        About Fate.

War is slipping, dripping death on earth.
If the child is father of the man,
Is the toy gun father of the Krupps?
        For Christ's sake think!
        While you sew
        Row after row.

Madeline Ida Bedford

MUNITION WAGES

Earning high wages? Yus,
  Five quid a week.
A woman, too, mind you,
  I calls it dim sweet.

Ye'are asking some questions –
  But bless yer, here goes:
I spends the whole racket
  On good times and clothes.

Me saving? Elijah!
  Yer do think I'm mad.
I'm acting the lady,
  But – I ain't living bad.

I'm having life's good times.
  See 'ere, it's like this:
The 'oof come o' danger,
  A touch-and-go bizz.

We're all here today, mate,
  Tomorrow – perhaps dead,
If Fate tumbles on us
  And blows up our shed.

Afraid! Are yer kidding?
  With money to spend!
Years back I wore tatters,
  Now – silk stockings, mi friend!

I've bracelets and jewellery,
  Rings envied by friends;
A sergeant to swank with,
  And something to lend.

I drive out in taxis,
  Do theatres in style.
And this is mi verdict –
  It is jolly worth while.

Worth while, for tomorrow
   If I'm blown to the sky,
I'll have repaid mi wages
   In death – and pass by.

THE PARSON'S JOB

What do you want
Coming to this 'ere 'ell?
Ain't it enough to know he's dead,
Killed by a bit o' German lead?
What! – the Lord means well?

I guess ye' are daft!
He's one o' the good'uns, Jim;
Nature's gentleman, rough but true.
He didn't know 'ow to sin,
But – what is that to you?

You make me sick.
Why should he die,
When forger Wright wins a V.C.
And criminal Kelly catches a spy?
That don't spell Justice to me.

Get out, or I'll strike you down.
I'm carrying his kid.
Do you call that fair?
Gawd – no wonder I wants to gib;
Our first-born, and his father – where?

You hold yer tongue.
What he said of our child
Ain't for you to be teaching me.
He called it 'Our little blossom wild'.
Why – can't yer let me be!

I hate your religion;
I don't want gold;
I only want my man.
What? It's in me to enfold
Jim in my babyland?

Gawd bless yer, Parson,
I'll try to think right
Upon my widowed way.
So Jim ain't quite out o' sight?
Teach me – ow – to pray.

FROM A TRENCH

Out here the dogs of war run loose,
   Their whipper-in is Death;
Across the spoilt and battered fields
   We hear their sobbing breath.
The fields where grew the living corn
   Are heavy with our dead;
Yet still the fields at home are green
   And I have heard it said:

              That –

There are crocuses at Nottingham!
Wild crocuses at Nottingham!
Blue crocuses at Nottingham!
Though here the grass is red.

There are little girls at Nottingham
   Who do not dread the Boche,
Young girls at school at Nottingham
   (Lord! how I need a wash!).
There are little boys at Nottingham
   Who never heard a gun;
There are silly fools at Nottingham
   Who think we're here for fun.

            When –
There are crocuses at Nottingham!
Young crocus buds at Nottingham!
Thousands of buds at Nottingham
Ungathered by the Hun.

But here we trample down the grass
   Into a purple slime;
There lives no tree to give the birds
   House room in pairing-time.
We live in holes, like cellar rats,
   But through the noise and smell

I often see those crocuses
  Of which the people tell.

           Why!
There are crocuses at Nottingham!
Bright crocuses at Nottingham!
Real crocuses at Nottingham!
Because we're here in Hell.

DRAFTS

Waking to darkness; early silence broken
By seagulls' cries, and something undefined
And far away. Through senses half-awoken,
A vague enquiry drifts into one's mind.
What's happening? Down the hill a movement quickens
And leaps to recognition round the turning –
Then one's heart wakes, and grasps the fact, and sickens –
'Are we down-hearted' . . . 'Keep the homefires burning'.
They go to God-knows-where, with songs of Blighty,
While I'm in bed, and ribbons in my nightie.

Sex, nothing more, constituent no greater
Than those which make an eyebrow's slant or fall,
In origin, sheer accident, which, later,
Decides the biggest differences of all.
And, through a war, involves the chance of death
Against a life of physical normality –
So dreadfully safe! O, damn the shibboleth
Of sex! God knows we've equal personality.
Why should men face the dark while women stay
To live and laugh and meet the sun each day.

They've gone. The drumming escort throbs the distance,
And down the hill the seagulls' cries are rife
And clamorous. But in their shrill persistence
I think they're telling me – 'We're all one Life'.
As much one life as when we flamed together,
As linked, as indivisible, as then;
When nothing's separate, does it matter whether
We live as women or we die as men?
Or swoop as seagulls! Everything is part
Of one supreme intent, the deathless heart.

Sybil Bristowe

OVER THE TOP

Ten more minutes! – Say yer prayers,
Read yer Bibles, pass the rum!
Ten more minutes! Strike me dumb,
'Ow they creeps on unawares,
Those blooming minutes. Nine. It's queer,
I'm sorter stunned. It ain't with fear!

Eight. It's like as if a frog
Waddled round in your inside,
Cold as ice-blocks, straddle wide,
Tired o' waiting. Where's the grog?
Seven. I'll play yer pitch and toss –
Six. – I wins, and tails yer loss.

'Nother minute sprinted by
'Fore I knowed it; only Four
(Break 'em into seconds) more
'Twixt us and Eternity.
Every word I've ever said
Seems a-shouting in my head.

Three. Larst night a little star
Fairly shook up in the sky,
Didn't like the lullaby
Rattled by the dogs of War.
Funny thing – that star all white
Saw old Blighty, too, larst night.

Two. I ain't ashamed o' prayers,
They're only wishes sent ter God
Bits o' plants from bloody sod
Trailing up His golden stairs.
Ninety seconds – Well, who cares!
One –
No fife, no blare, no drum –
Over the Top – to Kingdom Come!

Vera Brittain

THE LAMENT OF THE DEMOBILISED

'Four years,' some say consolingly. 'Oh well,
What's that? You're young. And then it must have been
A very fine experience for you!'
And they forget
How others stayed behind and just got on –
Got on the better since we were away.
And we came home and found
They had achieved, and men revered their names,
But never mentioned ours;
And no one talked heroics now, and we
Must just go back and start again once more.
'You threw four years into the melting-pot –
Did you indeed!' these others cry. 'Oh well,
The more fool you!'
And we're beginning to agree with them.

PERHAPS—

(To R.A.L. Died of Wounds in France, December 23rd, 1915)

Perhaps some day the sun will shine again,
    And I shall see that still the skies are blue,
And feel once more I do not live in vain,
    Although bereft of You.

Perhaps the golden meadows at my feet
    Will make the sunny hours of Spring seem gay,
And I shall find the white May blossoms sweet,
    Though You have passed away.

Perhaps the summer woods will shimmer bright,
    And crimson roses once again be fair,
And autumn harvest fields a rich delight,
    Although You are not there.

Perhaps some day I shall not shrink in pain
    To see the passing of the dying year,

And listen to the Christmas songs again,
    Although You cannot hear.

But, though kind Time may many joys renew,
    There is one greatest joy I shall not know
Again, because my heart for loss of You
    Was broken, long ago.

    1st London General Hospital
    February 1916

TO MY BROTHER*

(In Memory of July 1st, 1916)

Your battle-wounds are scars upon my heart,
    Received when in that grand and tragic 'show'
You played your part
    Two years ago,

And silver in the summer morning sun
    I see the symbol of your courage glow –
That Cross you won
    Two years ago.

Though now again you watch the shrapnel fly,
    And hear the guns that daily louder grow,
As in July
    Two years ago,

May you endure to lead the Last Advance
    And with your men pursue the flying foe
As once in France
    Two years ago.

* Captain E. H. Brittain, M.C. Written four days before his death in action in the Austrian offensive on the Italian Front, June 15th, 1918.

LAMPLIGHT

We planned to shake the world together, you and I
Being young, and very wise;
Now in the light of the green shaded lamp
Almost I see your eyes
Light with the old gay laughter; you and I
Dreamed greatly of an Empire in those days,
Setting our feet upon laborious ways,
And all you asked of fame
Was crossed swords in the Army List,
My Dear, against your name.

We planned a great Empire together, you and I,
Bound only by the sea;
Now in the quiet of a chill Winter's night
Your voice comes hushed to me
Full of forgotten memories: you and I
Dreamed great dreams of our future in those days,
Setting our feet on undiscovered ways,
And all I asked of fame
A scarlet cross on my breast, my Dear,
For the swords by your name.

We shall never shake the world together, you and I,
For you gave your life away;
And I think my heart was broken by the war,
Since on a summer day
You took the road we never spoke of: you and I
Dreamed greatly of an Empire in those days;
You set your feet upon the Western ways
And have no need of fame –
There's a scarlet cross on my breast, my Dear,
And a torn cross with your name.

December 1916

ROUEN

26 April–25 May 1915

Early morning over Rouen, hopeful, high, courageous morning,
And the laughter of adventure and the steepness of the stair,
And the dawn across the river, and the wind across the bridges,
And the empty littered station and the tired people there.

Can you recall those mornings and the hurry of awakening,
And the long-forgotten wonder if we should miss the way,
And the unfamiliar faces, and the coming of provisions,
And the freshness and the glory of the labour of the day?

Hot noontide over Rouen, and the sun upon the city,
Sun and dust unceasing, and the glare of cloudless skies,
And the voices of the Indians and the endless stream of soldiers,
And the clicking of the tatties, and the buzzing of the flies.

Can you recall those noontides and the reek of steam and coffee,
Heavy-laden noontides with the evening's peace to win,
And the little piles of Woodbines, and the sticky soda bottles,
And the crushes in the 'Parlour', and the letters coming in?

Quiet night-time over Rouen, and the station full of soldiers,
All the youth and pride of England from the ends of all the earth;
And the rifles piled together, and the creaking of the sword-belts,
And the faces bent above them, and the gay, heart-breaking
      mirth.

Can I forget the passage from the cool white-bedded Aid Post
Past the long sun-blistered coaches of the khaki Red Cross train
To the truck train full of wounded, and the weariness and
      laughter,
And 'Good-bye, and thank you, Sister', and the empty yards
      again?

Can you recall the parcels that we made them for the railroad,
Crammed and bulging parcels held together by their string,
And the voices of the sergeants who called the Drafts together,
And the agony and splendour when they stood to save the King?

Can you forget their passing, the cheering and the waving,
The little group of people at the doorway of the shed,
The sudden awful silence when the last train swung to darkness,
And the lonely desolation, and the mocking stars o'erhead?

Can you recall the midnights, and the footsteps of night
   watchers,
Men who came from darkness and went back to dark again,
And the shadows on the rail-lines and the all-inglorious labour,
And the promise of the daylight firing blue the window-pane?

Can you recall the passing through the kitchen door to morning,
Morning very still and solemn breaking slowly on the town,
And the early coastways engines that had met the ships at
   daybreak,
And the Drafts just out from England, and the day shift coming ·
   down?

Can you forget returning slowly, stumbling on the cobbles,
And the white-decked Red Cross barges dropping seawards for
   the tide,
And the search for English papers, and the blessed cool of water,
And the peace of half-closed shutters that shut out the world
   outside?

Can I forget the evenings and the sunsets on the island,
And the tall black ships at anchor far below our balcony,
And the distant call of bugles, and the white wine in the glasses,
And the long line of the street lamps, stretching Eastwards to the
   sea?

. . . When the world slips slow to darkness, when the office fire
   burns lower,
My heart goes out to Rouen, Rouen all the world away;
When other men remember I remember our Adventure
And the trains that go from Rouen at the ending of the day.

'SINCE THEY HAVE DIED'
Since they have died to give us gentleness,
And hearts kind with contentment and quiet mirth,
Let us who live give also happiness
And love, that's born of pity, to the earth.

For, I have thought, some day they may lie sleeping
Fogetting all the weariness and pain,
And smile to think their world is in our keeping,
And laughter come back to the earth again.

February 1916

LOVE, 1916
One said to me, 'Seek Love, for he is Joy
Called by another name'.
A Second said, 'Seek Love, for he is Power
Which is called Fame'.
Last said a Third, 'Seek Love, his name is Peace'.
I called him thrice,
And answer came, 'Love now
Is christened Sacrifice'.

August 1916

Isabel C. Clarke

ANNIVERSARY OF THE GREAT RETREAT
(1915)

Now a whole year has waxed and waned and whitened
   Over the mounds that marked that grim advance;
The winter snows have lain, the spring flowers brightened,
   On those belovèd graves of Northern France.

Caudry, Le Cateau, Landrécies, are written
   In our sad hearts with letters as of flame,
Where our young dead still lie, untimely smitten,
   In graves still unredeemed that bear no name.

And those who saw them spoke of the 'boy-faces'
   The English soldiers wore; they heard them sing
As they went forth to their appointed places,
   Who when night fell lay unremembering. . . .

O England, sing their fame in song and story,
   Who knew Death's victory not Life's defeat;
Be their names written on thy roll of glory,
   Who fought and perished in the Great Retreat!

These held thy high tradition in their keeping
   This flower of all a nation's youth and pride
And safe they hold it still in their last sleeping;
   They heard thy call and answered it and died. . . .

And by those graves that mark their proud surrender
   In days to come each one that lingereth
Shall sadly think of all their vanished splendour,
   'Contemptible', but faithful unto death.

So we press forward, step by step redeeming
   Each hallowed spot our dead have sanctified,
That we may whisper to them in their dreaming,
   The Victory is ours because you died. . . .

Margaret Postgate Cole

THE FALLING LEAVES
November 1915

Today, as I rode by,
I saw the brown leaves dropping from their tree
In a still afternoon,
When no wind whirled them whistling to the sky,
But thickly, silently,
They fell, like snowflakes wiping out the noon;
And wandered slowly thence
For thinking of a gallant multitude
Which now all withering lay,
Slain by no wind of age or pestilence,
But in their beauty strewed
Like snowflakes falling on the Flemish clay.

AFTERWARDS

Oh, my beloved, shall you and I
Ever be young again, be young again?
The people that were resigned said to me
– Peace will come and you will lie
Under the larches up in Sheer,
Sleeping,
And eating strawberries and cream and cakes –
        O cakes, O cakes, O cakes, from Fuller's!
And quite forgetting there's a train to town,
Plotting in an afternoon the new curves for the world.

And peace came. And lying in Sheer
I look round at the corpses of the larches
Whom they slew to make pit-props
For mining the coal for the great armies.
And think, a pit-prop cannot move in the wind,
Nor have red manes hanging in spring from its branches,
And sap making the warm air sweet.
Though you planted it out on the hill again it would be dead.

And if these years have made you into a pit-prop,
To carry the twisting galleries of the world's reconstruction
(Where you may thank God, I suppose
That they set you the sole stay of a nasty corner)
What use is it to you? What use
To have your body lying here
In Sheer, underneath the larches?

PRAEMATURI

When men are old, and their friends die,
They are not so sad,
Because their love is running slow,
And cannot spring from the wound with so sharp a pain;
And they are happy with many memories,
And only a little while to be alone.

But we are young, and our friends are dead
Suddenly, and our quick love is torn in two;
So our memories are only hopes that came to nothing.
We are left alone like old men; we should be dead
— But there are years and years in which we shall still be young.

THE VETERAN
May, 1916

We came upon him sitting in the sun,
    Blinded by war, and left. And past the fence
There came young soldiers from the Hand and Flower,
    Asking advice of his experience.

And he said this, and that, and told them tales,
    And all the nightmares of each empty head
Blew into air; then, hearing us beside,
    'Poor chaps, how'd they know what it's like?' he said.

And we stood there, and watched him as he sat,
   Turning his sockets where they went away,
Until it came to one of us to ask
   'And you're – how old?'
       'Nineteen, the third of May.'

WOMEN AT MUNITION MAKING

Their hands should minister unto the flame of life,
    Their fingers guide
The rosy teat, swelling with milk,
To the eager mouth of the suckling babe
Or smooth with tenderness,
    Softly and soothingly,
The heated brow of the ailing child.
Or stray among the curls
Of the boy or girl, thrilling to mother love.
    But now,
Their hands, their fingers
Are coarsened in munition factories.
Their thoughts, which should fly
Like bees among the sweetest mind flowers,
Gaining nourishment for the thoughts to be,
Are bruised against the law,
    'Kill, kill'.
They must take part in defacing and destroying the natural body
Which, certainly during this dispensation
Is the shrine of the spirit.
    O God!
Throughout the ages we have seen,
    Again and again
    Men by Thee created
    Cancelling each other.
And we have marvelled at the seeming annihilation
    Of Thy work.
But this goes further,
    Taints the fountain head,
Mounts like a poison to the Creator's very heart.
    O God!
Must It anew be sacrificed on earth?

FALLEN

He was wounded and he fell in the midst of hoarse shouting.
The tide passed, and the waves came and whispered about his
    ankles.
Far off he heard a cock crow – children laughing,
Rising at dawn to greet the storm of petals
Shaken from apple-boughs; he heard them cry,
And turned again to find the breast of her,
And sank confusèd with a little sigh . . .
Thereafter water running, and a voice
That seemed to stir and flutter through the trenches
And set dead lips to talking . . .

Wreckage was mingled with the storm of petals . . .

He felt her near him, and the weight dropped off –
    Suddenly . . .

ZEPPELINS

I saw the people climbing up the street
Maddened with war and strength and thought to kill;
And after followed Death, who held with skill
His torn rags royally, and stamped his feet.

The fires flamed up and burnt the serried town,
Most where the sadder, poorer houses were;
Death followed with proud feet and smiling stare,
And the mad crowds ran madly up and down.

And many died and hid in unfound places
In the black ruins of the frenzied night;
And Death still followed in his surplice, white
And streaked in imitation of their faces.

.   .   .

But in the morning men began again
To mock Death following in bitter pain.

Elizabeth Daryush

FLANDERS FIELDS

Here the scanted daisy glows
Glorious as the carmined rose;
Here the hill-top's verdure mean
Fair is with unfading green;
Here, where sorrow still must tread,
All her graves are garlanded.

And still, O glad passer-by
Of the fields of agony,
Lower laughter's voice, and bare
Thy head in the valley where
Poppies bright and rustling wheat
Are a desert to love's feet.

FOR A SURVIVOR OF THE MESOPOTAMIAN
CAMPAIGN

War's wasted era is a desert shore,
As know those who have passèd there, a place
Where, within sound of swoll'n destruction's roar,
Wheel the wild vultures, lust and terror base;
Where, making ready for them, stalk the grim
Barbarian forms, hunger, disease and pain,
Who, slashing all life's beauty limb from limb,
Crush it as folly on their stony plain.

A desert: – those too who, as thou, have been
Followers of war's angel, Sacrifice,
(Stern striders to beyond brute torment's scene,
Soarers above the swerves of fear and vice)
Know that the lightning of his ghostly gaze
Has wrecked for them for ever earth's small ways.

SUBALTERNS

She said to one: 'How glows
My heart at the hot thought
Of battle's glorious throes!'
He said: 'For us who fought
Are icy memories
That must for ever freeze
The sunny hours they bought.'

She said to one: 'How light
Must be your freed heart now,
After the heavy fight!'
He said: 'Well, I don't know . . .
The war gave one a shake,
Somehow, knocked one awake . . .
Now, life's so deadly slow.'

UNKNOWN WARRIOR

Not that broad path chose he, which whoso wills
May tread, if he but pay the fatal price,
And for such sweets as earthly life extils,
Slaughter his heaven-born soul in sacrifice.

But he, though loving these, cast yet with strong
Hand all aside, and took the obscure way,
Which few may find, or, finding, follow long, –
O let not weak regrets hinder me, nay,

Health, wealth, fame, friendship, all that I hold dear,
I'll spend, nor seek return. O what dark crown
Be his, he cares not, who thus gives; how near
May hang yet his lost laurels of renown:

Yea, who dares thus die, haply he may see,
Suddenly, unsought immortality.

AFTER BOURLON WOOD

In one of London's most exclusive haunts,
Amid the shining lights and table ware,
We sat, where meagre Mistress Ration flaunts
Herself in syncopated music there.

He was a Major twenty-six years old,
Back from the latest party of the Hun,
He said: 'The beastly blighters had me bowled
Almost before the picnic had begun.

'By Jove! I was particularly cross,
I had looked forward to a little fling!
(These censored wine lists have me at a loss.)
But what have you been doing, dear old thing?'

'I go to bed,' I said, 'at half-past ten,
And lead the life of any simple Waac –
Alas! a meatless, sweetless one – and then
I have a little joy when you come back.

'But mostly life is dull upon this isle,
And is inclined to be a trifle limp.'
'I hate,' he said, 'the Hun to cramp my style,
We'll try and give it just a little crimp.'

'On Saturday,' I cried, 'we stop at one:
To help you with the crimping would be grand!'
'Sorry,' he said, 'it simply can't be done,
I've got a most unpleasant job on hand.'

'Unpleasant job!' I asked. 'What do you mean?'
'I would,' he said, 'avoid it if I could,
But Georgius Rex, it seems, is awfully keen
To give me the M.C. for being good.'

29

LONDON IN WAR

White faces,
Like helpless petals on the stream,
Swirl by,
Or linger
And then go. . . .

Ancient summer burns
Where green trees branch
From palaces of stone;
I see the brightness
Through a throbbing gloom,
While death rattles
To a tripping melody. . . .

Hot laughter comes,
With tears of ice,
Where War is God
And God is War;
For He has torn
The gallant spirits that He gave,
Till joy is agony,
And agony is joy. . . .

Night falls with its olden touch,
But sleep comes
Like a bloody man,
And the stars
Are wounded birds
That fall
For ever. . . .

PLUCK

Crippled for life at seventeen,
   His great eyes seem to question why:
With both legs smashed it might have been
    Better in that grim trench to die
    Than drag maimed years out helplessly.

A child – so wasted and so white,
   He told a lie to get his way,
To march, a man with men, and fight
    While other boys are still at play.
    A gallant lie your heart will say.

So broke with pain, he shrinks in dread
   To see the 'dresser' drawing near;
And winds the clothes about his head
    That none may see his heart-sick fear.
    His shaking, strangled sobs you hear.

But when the dreaded moment's there
   He'll face us all, a soldier yet,
Watch his bared wounds with unmoved air,
    (Though tell-tale lashes still are wet),
    And smoke his woodbine cigarette.

GRAMOPHONE TUNES

Through the long ward the gramophone
   Grinds out its nasal melodies:
'Where did you get that girl?' it shrills.
    The patients listen at their ease,
Through clouds of strong tobacco-smoke:
    The gramophone can always please.

The Welsh boy has it by his bed,
   (He's lame – one leg was blown away).
He'll lie propped up with pillows there,

And wind the handle half the day.
His neighbour, with the shattered arm,
    Picks out the records he must play.

Jock with his crutches beats the time;
    The gunner, with his head close-bound,
Listens with puzzled, patient smile:
    (Shell-shock – he cannot hear a sound).
The others join in from their beds,
    And send the chorus rolling round.

Somehow for me these common tunes
    Can never sound the same again:
They've magic now to thrill my heart
    And bring before me, clear and plain,
Man that is master of his flesh,
    And has the laugh of death and pain.

NIGHT DUTY

The pain and laughter of the day are done,
So strangely hushed and still the long ward seems,
Only the Sister's candle softly beams.
Clear from the church near by the clock strikes 'one';
And all are wrapt away in secret sleep and dreams.

They bandied talk and jest from bed to bed;
Now sleep has touched them with a subtle change.
They lie here deep withdrawn, remote and strange;
A dimly outlined shape, a tumbled head.
Through what far lands do now their wand'ring spirits range?

Here one cries sudden on a sobbing breath,
Gripped in the clutch of some incarnate fear:
What terror through the darkness draweth near?
What memory of carnage and of death?
What vanished scenes of dread to his closed eyes appear?

And one laughs out with an exultant joy.
An athlete he – Maybe his young limbs strain
In some remembered game, and not in vain
To win his side the goal – Poor crippled boy,
Who in the waking world will never run again.

One murmurs soft and low a woman's name;
And here a vet'ran soldier, calm and still
As sculptured marble sleeps, and roams at will
Through eastern lands where sunbeams scorch like flame,
By rich bazaar and town, and wood-wrapt snow-crowned hill.

Through the wide open window one great star,
Swinging her lamp above the pear-tree high,
Looks in upon these dreaming forms that lie
So near in body, yet in soul as far
As those bright worlds thick strewn on that vast depth of sky.

A VOLUNTEER

He had no heart for war, its ways and means,
Its train of machinations and machines,
Its murky provenance, its flagrant ends;
His soul, unpledged for his own dividends,
He had not ventured for a nation's spoils.
So had he sighed for England in her toils
Of greed, was't like his pulse would beat less blithe
To see·the Teuton shells on Rotherhithe
And Mayfair — so each body had 'scaped its niche,
The wretched poor, the still more wretched rich?
Why had he sought the struggle and its pain?
Lest little girls with linked hands in the lane
Should look 'You did not shield us!' as they wended
Across his window when the war was ended.

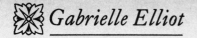

PIERROT GOES TO WAR

In the sheltered garden, pale beneath the moon,
(Drenched with swaying fragrance, redolent with June!)
There, among the shadows, some one lingers yet –
Pierrot, the lover, parts from Pierrette.

Bugles, bugles, bugles, blaring down the wind,
Sound the flaming challenge – *Leave your dreams behind!*
Come away from shadows, turn your back on June –
Pierrot, go forward to face the golden noon!

In the muddy trenches, black and torn and still,
(How the charge swept over, to break against the hill!)
Huddled in the shadows, boyish figures lie –
They whom Death, saluting, called upon to die.

Bugles, ghostly bugles, whispering down the wind –
Dreams too soon are over, gardens left behind.
Only shadows linger, for love does not forget –
Pierrot goes forward – but what of Pierrette?

October, 1917

EASTER MONDAY
(In Memoriam E.T.)

In the last letter that I had from France
You thanked me for the silver Easter egg
Which I had hidden in the box of apples
You liked to munch beyond all other fruit.
You found the egg the Monday before Easter,
And said, 'I will praise Easter Monday now –
It was such a lovely morning'. Then you spoke
Of the coming battle and said, 'This is the eve.
Good-bye. And may I have a letter soon.'

That Easter Monday was a day for praise,
It was such a lovely morning. In our garden
We sowed our earliest seeds, and in the orchard
The apple-bud was ripe. It was the eve.
There are three letters that you will not get.

April 9th, 1917

PEACE
I

I am as awful as my brother War,
I am the sudden silence after clamour.
I am the face that shows the seamy scar
When blood has lost its frenzy and its glamour.
Men in my pause shall know the cost at last
That is not to be paid in triumphs or tears,
Men will begin to judge the thing that's past
As men will judge it in a hundred years.

Nations! whose ravenous engines must be fed
Endlessly with the father and the son,
My naked light upon your darkness, dread! –
By which ye shall behold what ye have done:

Whereon, more like a vulture than a dove,
Ye set my seal in hatred, not in love.

II

Let no man call me good. I am not blest.
My single virtue is the end of crimes,
I only am the period of unrest,
The ceasing of the horrors of the times;
My good is but the negative of ill,
Such ill as bends the spirit with despair,
Such ill as makes the nations' soul stand still
And freeze to stone beneath its Gorgon glare.

Be blunt, and say that peace is but a state
Wherein the active soul is free to move,
And nations only show as mean or great
According to the spirit then they prove. –
O which of ye whose battle-cry is Hate
Will first in peace dare shout the name of Love?

'NOW THAT YOU TOO'

Now that you too must shortly go the way
Which in these bloodshot years uncounted men
Have gone in vanishing armies day by day,
And in their numbers will not come again:
I must not strain the moments of our meeting
Striving each look, each accent, not to miss,
Or question of our parting and our greeting,
Is this the last of all? is this – or this?

Last sight of all it may be with these eyes,
Last touch, last hearing, since eyes, hands, and ears,
Even serving love, are our mortalities,
And cling to what they own in mortal fears: –
But oh, let end what will, I hold you fast
By immortal love, which has no first or last.

S. Gertrude Ford

'A FIGHT TO A FINISH'

'Fight the year out!' the War-lords said:
What said the dying among the dead?

'To the last man!' cried the profiteers:
What said the poor in the starveling years?

'War is good!' yelled the Jingo-kind:
What said the wounded, the maimed and blind?

'Fight on!' the Armament-kings besought:
Nobody asked what the women thought.

'On!' echoed Hate where the fiends kept tryst:
Asked the Church, even, what said Christ?

NATURE IN WAR-TIME

The banished thrush, the homeless rook
    Share now the human exile's woe.
Mourns not that forest felled, which took
        Three hundred years to grow?

Grieve not those meadows scarred and cleft,
    Mined with deep holes and reft of grass,
Gardens where not a flower is left,
        Fouled streams, once clear as glass?

And yon green vale where Spring was found
    Laughing among her daffodils . . .
Winds sweep it now; a battle-ground
        Between two gun-swept hills.

THE TENTH ARMISTICE DAY
I

'Lest we forget!' Let us remember, then,
    How England cheered – sang – shouted, in the glow

Of a fog-shrouded sun ten years ago;
How Peace rose, like a dim star on a fen.
And yet, so short the memories of men,
    Do we indeed remember War laid low,
    Peace brought, by one great man* at one great blow,
Dealt by one clarion voice and golden pen?

Surely his voice comes borne to us with theirs
    Who fell – the voice of husband, brother, father,
Lover and son: 'Spend not on us your cares,
    Your wreaths, for we have better flowers to gather.
But lift the load our workless comrade bears:
    Flowers for the dead? Bread for the living rather!'

II

And yet bring flowers and heap them, all this day,
    On the high Cenotaph, memorial-wise,
    So to commemorate their sacrifice:
No flowers can be more beautiful than they.
Let the red rose of England burn alway,
    And amaranth, for their life that never dies,
    And poppies reddening round, where laurel lies
Also. Yet more they ask; yet more they may.

Give, give the pyramid its cope and crown
    In the olive-leaf, the Peace dove's silver glitter,
    Flying above the red flood's desolations!
They warred to end war: to fulfil their hope
    Give them a better monument and fitter;
        Build their memorial in the League of Nations!

*President Wilson.

THE THREE LADS

Down the road rides a German lad,
    Into the distance grey;
Straight toward the north as a bullet flies,
The dusky north, with its cold, sad skies;
But the song that he sings is merry and glad,
    For he's off to the war and away.
'Then hey! for our righteous king!' (he cries)
'And the good old God in his good old skies!
And ho! for love and a pair of blue eyes, –
    For I'm off to the war and away!'

Down the road rides a Russian lad,
    Into the distance grey,
Out toward the glare of the steppes he spurs,
And he hears the wolves in the southern firs;
But the song that he sings is blithe and glad,
    For he's off to the war and away.
'Then hey! for our noble tzar!' (he cries)
'And liberty that never dies!
And ho! for love and a pair of blue eyes, –
    For I'm off to the war and away!'

Down the road rides an English lad,
    Into the distance grey.
Through the murk and fog of the river's breath,
Through the dank, dark night he rides to his death;
But the song that he sings is gay and glad,
    For he's off to the war and away.
'Then hey! for our honest king!' (he cries)
'And hey! for truth, and down with lies!
And ho! for love and a pair of blue eyes, –
    For I'm off to the war and away!'

Lillian Gard

HER 'ALLOWANCE'!

'Er looked at me bunnet (I knows 'e ain't noo!)
'Er turned up 'er nose at the patch on me shoe!
And 'er sez, pointed like, 'Liza, what do 'e do
        With yer 'llowance?'

'Er looked at the children (they'm clean and they'm neat,
But their clothes be as plain as the victuals they eat):
And 'er sez, 'Why not dress 'em up fine for a treat
        With yer 'llowance?'

I sees 'er long feather and trimmy-up gown:
I sez, as I looks 'er quite square up and down,
'Do 'e think us keeps 'oliday 'ere in the town
        With my 'llowance?

'Not likely!' I sez. And I bids 'er 'Good-day!'
And I kneels on the shabby old canvas to pray
For Bill, who's out fightin' such brave miles away.
(And I puts back a foo o' they coins for 'e may
Be needin' a part – may my Bill – who can say? –
        Of my 'llowance!)

Muriel Elsie Graham

THE LARK ABOVE THE TRENCHES

'A French soldier writing to *Le Matin* says that the other day a lark sang above the trenches its spring song, which was to them a song of joy and hope.' – February 1915

All day the guns had worked their hellish will,
        And all night long
With sobbing breath men gasped their lives away,
Or shivered restless on the ice-cold clay,
    Till morn broke pale and chill
        With sudden song.

Above the sterile furrows war had ploughed
        With deep-trenched seams,
Wherein this year such bitter seed is sown,
Wherein this year no fruitful grain is strown,
    A lark poured from the cloud
        Its throbbing dreams.

It sang – and pain and death were passing shows –
        So glad and strong;
Life soared triumphant, though a myriad men
Were swept like leaves beyond the living's ken,
    That wounded hope arose
        To greet that song.

THE BATTLE OF THE SWAMPS

Across the blinded lowlands the beating rain blows chill,
The trenched earth turns to water, the shell-holes ooze and fill,
A tragic land where little that's sweet or sane survives –
O hungry swamps of Flanders that swallow up men's lives!

O numbing nights of Flanders, whose cold breath cannot quench
The grim enduring courage that holds each mud-fouled trench,
That struggles stiffly forward to meet the shattering guns –
O bitter swamps of Flanders that rob us of our sons!

Yet in the sheltered homeland that lies such worlds away,
What shrinking hearts are braving that suffocating clay!
And when on roof and window the rain beats, then – O then,
O deathless swamps of Flanders, our hearts are with our men.

THE WYKHAMIST

In the wake of the yellow sunset one pale star
Hangs over the darkening city's purple haze.
An errand-boy in the street beneath me plays
On a penny whistle. Very faint and far
Comes the scroop of tortured gear on a battered car.
A hyacinth nods pallid blooms on the window sill,
Swayed by the tiny wind. St Catherine's Hill
Is a place of mystery, a land of dreams.
The tramp of soldiers, barrack-marching, seems
A thing remote, untouched by fate or time.
. . . A year ago you heard Cathedral's chime,
You hurried up to books – a year ago;
– Shouted for 'Houses' in New Field below.
. . . You . . . 'died of wounds' . . . they told me

                       . . . yet your feet
Pass with the others down the twilit street.

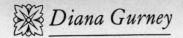 *Diana Gurney*

THE FALLEN

Shall we not lay our holly wreath
Here at the foot of this high cross?
We do not know, perhaps a breath
Of our remembering may come
To them at last where they are sleeping,
They are quiet, they are dumb,
No more of mirth, no more of weeping,
Silent Christmas they are keeping;
Ours the sorrow, ours the loss.

NON-COMBATANT

Before one drop of angry blood was shed
    I was sore hurt and beaten to my knee;
Before one fighting man reeled back and died
    The War-Lords struck at me.

They struck me down – an idle, useless mouth,
    As cumbrous – nay, more cumbrous – than the dead,
With life and heart afire to give and give
    I take a dole instead.

With life and heart afire to give and give
    I take and eat the bread of charity.
In all the length of all this eager land,
    No man has need of me.

That is my hurt – my burning, beating wound;
    That is the spear-thrust driven through my pride!
With aimless hands, and mouth that must be fed,
    I wait and stand aside.

Let me endure it, then, with stiffened lip:
    I, even I, have suffered in the strife!
Let me endure it then – I give my pride
    Where others give a life.

Helen Hamilton

THE GHOULS

You strange old ghouls,
Who gloat with dulled old eyes,
   Over those lists,
   Those dreadful lists,
   To see what name
   Of friend, relation,
   However distant,
   May be appended
To your private Roll of Honour.
Unknowingly you draw, it seems,
   From their young bodies,
   Dead young bodies,
   Fresh life,
   New value,
Now that yours are ebbing.
   You strange old ghouls,
Who gloat with dulled old eyes,
   Over those lists,
   Those dreadful lists,
   Of young men dead.

THE JINGO-WOMAN

Jingo-woman
(How I dislike you!)
Dealer in white feathers,
Insulter, self-appointed,
Of all the men you meet,
Not dressed in uniform,
When to your mind,
      (A sorry mind),
      They should be,
      The test?
The judgment of your eye,
That wild, infuriate eye,

Whose glance, so you declare,
      Reveals unerringly,
Who's good for military service.
Oh! exasperating woman,
I'd like to wring your neck,
      I really would!
            You make all women seem such duffers!
            Besides exemptions,
            Enforced and held reluctantly,
            – Not that you'll believe it –
            You *must* know surely
Men there are, and young men too,
Physically not fit to serve,
Who look in their civilian garb
      Quite stout and hearty.
And most of whom, I'll wager,
Have been rejected several times.
How keen, though, your delight,
      Keen and malignant,
Should one offer you his seat,
      In crowded bus or train,
Thus giving you the chance to say,
In cold, incisive tones of scorn:
      'No, I much prefer to stand
      As you, young man, are not in khaki!'
Heavens! I wonder you're alive!
      Oh, these men,
These twice-insulted men,
      What iron self-control they show.
      What wonderful forbearance!

But still the day may come
For you to prove yourself
As sacrificial as upbraiding.
So far they are not taking us
But if the war goes on much longer
      They might,

Nay more,
They must,
When the last man has gone.
And if and when that dark day dawns,
You'll join up first, of course,
Without waiting to be fetched.
But in the meantime,
Do hold your tongue!
You shame us women.
Can't you see it isn't decent,
To flout and goad men into doing,
What is not asked of you?

THE ROMANCING POET

Granted that you write verse,
Much better verse than I,
(Which isn't saying much!)
I wish you would refrain
From making glad romance
Of this most hideous war.
It has no glamour,
Save man's courage,
His indomitable spirit,
His forgetfulness of self!
If you have words –
Fit words, I mean,
Not your usual stock-in-trade,
Of tags and *clichés* –
To hymn such greatness,
Use them.
But have you?
Anyone can babble.
If you must wax descriptive,
Do get the background right,
A little right!

Helen Hamilton

The blood, the filth, the horrors,
Suffering on such a scale,
That you and I, try as we may,
        Can only faintly vision it.
Don't make a pretty song about it!
        It is an insult to the men,
        Doomed to be crucified each day,
        For us at home!
Abstain too, if you can,
From bidding us to plume ourselves
For being of the self-same breed
        As these heroic souls,
With the obvious implication,
We have the right to take the credit,
        Vicarious credit,
        For their immortal deeds!
        What next?
        It is an outrage!
        We are not glory-snatchers!

Ada M. Harrison

NEW YEAR, 1916

Those that go down into silence . . .

There is no silence in their going down,
  Although their grave-turf is not wet with tears,
Although Grief passes by them, and Renown
  Has garnered them no glory for the years.

The cloud of war moves on, and men forget
  That empires fall. We go our heedless ways
Unknowing still, uncaring still, and yet
  The very dust is clamorous with their praise.

AN INCIDENT

He was just a boy, as I could see,
For he sat in the tent there close by me.
I held the lamp with its flickering light,
And felt the hot tears blur my sight
As the doctor took the blood-stained bands
From both his brave, shell-shattered hands –
His boy hands, wounded more pitifully
Than Thine, O Christ, on Calvary.

I was making tea in the tent where they,
The wounded, came in their agony;
And the boy turned when his wounds were dressed,
Held up his face like a child at the breast,
Turned and held his tired face up,
For he could not hold the spoon or cup,
And I fed him. . . . Mary, Mother of God,
All women tread where thy feet have trod.

And still on the battlefield of pain
Christ is stretched on His Cross again;
And the Son of God in agony hangs,
Womanhood striving to ease His pangs.
For each son of man is a son divine,
Not just to the mother who calls him 'mine',
As he stretches out his stricken hand,
Wounded to death for the Mother Land.

AIRMAN, R.F.C.

He heard them in the silence of the night
Whirring and thudding through the moonlit sky
And wondered where their target, pondered why . . .
Unsleeping, saw again with a young sight
The docks, yards, aerodromes revealed and white,
Heard the guns crack, saw searchlights sidle by,
Felt the bombs fall, the débris mounting high,
Knew the earth blazing and the skies alight . . .

They had his task; they did what he had done:
Their youth – as his – by battle was hemmed round:
Their lives hung on a thread – how finely spun! –
(Little they cared as on their way they wound!) . . .
He prayed they might come safely through, each one,
And find a better world than he had found.

THE SEED-MERCHANT'S SON

The Seed-Merchant has lost his son,
His dear, his loved, his only one.

So young he was. Even now it seems
He was a child with a child's dreams.

He would race over the meadow-bed
With his bright, bright eyes and his cheeks all red.

Fair and healthy and long of limb:
It made one young just to look at him.

His school books, into the cupboard thrust,
Have scarcely had time to gather dust.

Died in the war. . . . And it seems his eyes
Must have looked at death with a child's surprise.

. . .

The Seed-Merchant goes on his way:
I saw him out on his land today;

Old to have fathered so young a son,
And now the last glint of his youth is gone.

What could one say to him in his need?
Little there seemed to say indeed.

So still he was that the birds flew round
The grey of his head without a sound,

Careless and tranquil in the air,
As if naught human were standing there.

.   .   .

Oh, never a soul could understand
Why he looked at the earth, and the seed in his hand,

As he had never before seen seed or sod:
I heard him murmur: 'Thank God, thank God!'

May Herschel-Clarke

'FOR VALOUR'

Jest bronze – you wouldn't ever know,
To see it jest a-lying there,
It's really made o' golden hair,
And firm young flesh as white as snow.
No gold, nor none o' them art tones –
Only two 'ands and willing feet,
A sturdy form, a young 'eart's beat,
Two gay, bright eyes – jest blood and bones . . .
My blood and bones, *my* 'eart. . . . Ah! well,
They wrote to tell me it was fine
To see the way he laid that mine,
So brave and smiling . . . then he fell. . . .
There never was no 'olding 'im,
And there it must 'a' bin the same.
But, 'fore he . . . went . . . he called my name. . . .
Eh, but it makes my old eyes dim
To think I was so far away. . . .
Yes, that's 'is photo. Look at it.
Say, don't you think I've done my bit? . . .
Jest bronze. . . . *Gawd! What a price to pay!*

'NOTHING TO REPORT'

One minute we was laughin', me an' Ted,
The next, he lay beside me grinnin' – dead.
'There's nothin' to report,' the papers said.

A WAR FILM

I saw,
With a catch of the breath and the heart's uplifting,
Sorrow and pride,
    The 'week's great draw' –
The Mons Retreat;
The 'Old Contemptibles' who fought, and died,
The horror and the anguish and the glory.

As in a dream,
Still hearing machine-guns rattle and shells scream,
I came out into the street.

When the day was done,
My little son
Wondered at bath-time why I kissed him so,
Naked upon my knee.
How could he know
The sudden terror that assaulted me? . . .
The body I had borne
Nine moons beneath my heart,
A part of me . . .
If, someday,
It should be taken away
To War. Tortured. Torn.
Slain.
Rotting in No Man's Land, out in the rain –
My little son . . .
Yet all those men had mothers, every one.

How should he know
Why I kissed and kissed and kissed him, crooning his name?
He thought that I was daft.
He thought it was a game,
And laughed, and laughed.

DULCE ET DECORUM?

We buried of our dead the dearest one —
Said each to other, 'Here then let him lie,
And they may find the place, when all is done,
From the old may tree standing guard near by.'

Strong limbs whereon the wasted life blood dries,
And soft cheeks that a girl might wish her own,
A scholar's brow, o'ershadowing valiant eyes,
Henceforth shall pleasure charnel-worms alone.

For we, that loved him, covered up his face,
And laid him in the sodden earth away,
And left him lying in that lonely place
To rot and moulder with the mouldering clay.

The hawthorn that above his grave head grew
Like an old crone toward the raw earth bowed,
Wept softly over him, the whole night through,
And made him of her tears a glimmering shroud.

. . .

Oh Lord of Hosts, no hallowed prayer we bring,
Here for Thy grace is no importuning,
No room for those that will not strive nor cry
When lovingkindness with our dead lies slain:
    Give us our fathers' heathen hearts again,
    Valour to dare, and fortitude to die.

REPORTED MISSING

My thought shall never be that you are dead:
Who laughed so lately in this quiet place.
The dear and deep-eyed humour of that face
Held something ever living, in Death's stead.
Scornful I hear the flat things they have said
And all their piteous platitudes of pain.
I laugh! I laugh! – For you will come again –
This heart would never beat if you were dead.
The world's adrowse in twilight hushfulness,
There's purple lilac in your little room,
And somewhere out beyond the evening gloom
Small boys are culling summer watercress.
Of these familiar things I have no dread
Being so very sure you are not dead.

THE LOST ARMY

('The 1/5 Norfolks . . . consisting of 16 officers and 250 men
. . . charged into a wood . . . not one of them came out
again.' *Sir Ian Hamilton's Suvla Bay despatch, 1916*)

Singing and shouting they swept to the treacherous forest
Darkness and silence received them and smothered their pain
Darkness and silence and night is the end of their story –
They came not again!

Never a hero came forth of the legions that entered
Never a cry nor a prayer, nor a song of the brave
Dark and in silence the sinister forest received them
And made them a grave!

Somewhere deep down in the heart of the wood that betrayed
 them
Shoulder to shoulder they lie, with their wounds to the fore
There in the dark and the silence they sleep, the Lost Army
Returning no more.

We may not hear of their valour, their death or their glory
Nay! They were ours – and they died for their country, and so
Darkness and silence and night is the end of their story –
All we need know.

1916

TRANSPORT OF WOUNDED IN
MESOPOTAMIA, 1917

You who sat safe at home
And let us die
You who said 'all was well'
And knew the lie. . . .
(Fever and flies and sand
Sand and fever and flies
Till the end of each weary day
Saw the wearier night arise!)

You who sat safe at home
        And let us die!

Sun in our hopeless eyes
As the crawling barges plied
On the waveless, treacly tide –
        (Sand and fever and flies
        Flies and fever and sand
        Till we smiled at our good friend Death
        When he shook us by the hand!)
When we dreamt of rest and care –
But the mirage flitted away
And day after tortured day
Closed – in the same despair!

        Hush, and bury it deep –
        Bury us side by side!
        Shuffle the cards again
        Juggle – 'regret' and 'explain' –
        You – for whose fault we died!

We who lie far away
        God! Hear our cry
Upon Their hands our blood
        Is yet undry
Those who sat safe at Home
        And let us die!

CASUALTY

John Delaney of the Rifles has been shot.
   A man we never knew,
   Does it cloud the day for you
   That he lies among the dead
Moving, hearing, heeding not?

No history will hold his humble name.
   No sculptured stone will tell
   The traveller where he fell;
   That he lies among the dead
Is the measure of his fame.

When our troops return victorious shall we care
   That deaf to all the cheers,
   Lacking tribute of our tears,
   He is lying with the dead
Stark and silent, God knows where?

John Delaney of the Rifles – who was he?
   A name seen on a list
   All unknown and all unmissed.
   What to us that he is dead? –
Yet he died for you and me.

THE DESERTER

There was a man, – don't mind his name,
Whom Fear had dogged by night and day.
He could not face the German guns
And so he turned and ran away.
Just that – he turned and ran away,
But who can judge him, you or I?
God makes a man of flesh and blood
Who yearns to live and not to die.
And this man when he feared to die
Was scared as any frightened child,

His knees were shaking under him,
His breath came fast, his eyes were wild.
I've seen a hare with eyes as wild,
With throbbing heart and sobbing breath.
But oh! it shames one's soul to see
A man in abject fear of death.
But fear had gripped him, so had death;
His number had gone up that day,
They might not heed his frightened eyes,
They shot him when the dawn was grey.
Blindfolded, when the dawn was grey,
He stood there in a place apart,
The shots rang out and down he fell,
An English bullet in his heart.
An English bullet in his heart!
But here's the irony of life, –
His mother thinks he fought and fell
A hero, foremost in the strife.
So she goes proudly; to the strife
Her best, her hero son she gave.
O well for her she does not know
He lies in a deserter's grave.

SCREENS

(In a Hospital)

They put the screens around his bed;
   A crumpled heap I saw him lie,
White counterpane and rough dark head,
   Those screens – they showed that he would die.

They put the screens about his bed;
   We might not play the gramophone,
And so we played at cards instead
   And left him dying there alone.

The covers on the screen are red,
    The counterpanes are white and clean; –
He might have lived and loved and wed
    But now he's done for at nineteen.

An ounce or more of Turkish lead,
    He got his wounds at Suvla Bay;
They've brought the Union Jack to spread
    Upon him when he goes away.

He'll want those three red screens no more,
    Another man will get his bed,
We'll make the row we did before
    But – Jove! – I'm sorry that he's dead.

WHAT REWARD?
You gave your life, boy,
    And *you* gave a limb:
But he who gave his precious wits,
    Say, what reward for him?

One has his glory,
    One has found his rest.
But what of this poor babbler here
    With chin sunk on his breast?

Flotsam of battle,
    With brain bemused and dim,
O God, for such a sacrifice
    Say, what reward for him?

Olive E. Lindsay

DESPAIR

Half of me died at Bapaume,
  And the rest of me is a log:
For my soul was in the other half;
  And the half that is here is a clog
On the one who would always be doing
  In days never to come again.
Carry me into the darkness, sir,
  And put me out of my pain.

The best of me died at Bapaume
  When the world went up in fire,
And the soul that was mine deserted
  And left me, a thing in the mire,
With a madden'd and dim remembrance
  Of a time when my life was whole.
Carry me into the darkness, sir,
  And let me find my soul.

If half of you went at Bapaume,
  And with it your soul went too,
That soul has laid as a sacrifice
  The half that was torn from you.
At the feet of the One who Himself has given,
  Laid all that a man can give;
And then will return to the other half
  And show it how to live.

Amy Lowell

CONVALESCENCE

From out the dragging vastness of the sea,
   Wave-fettered, bound in sinuous seaweed strands,
   He toils toward the rounding beach, and stands
One moment, white and dripping, silently,
Cut like a cameo in lazuli,
   Then falls, betrayed by shifting shells, and lands
   Prone in the jeering water, and his hands
Clutch for support where no support can be.
   So up, and down, and forward, inch by inch,
He gains upon the shore, where poppies glow
And sandflies dance their little lives away.
   The sucking waves retard, and tighter clinch
The weeds about him, but the land-winds blow,
And in the sky there blooms the sun of May.

Rose Macaulay

PICNIC

July 1917

We lay and ate sweet hurt-berries
    In the bracken of Hurt Wood.
Like a quire of singers singing low
    The dark pines stood.

Behind us climbed the Surrey hills,
    Wild, wild in greenery;
At our feet the downs of Sussex broke
    To an unseen sea.

And life was bound in a still ring,
    Drowsy, and quiet, and sweet . . .
When heavily up the south-east wind
    The great guns beat.

We did not wince, we did not weep,
    We did not curse or pray;
We drowsily heard, and someone said,
    'They sound clear today'.

We did not shake with pity and pain,
    Or sicken and blanch white.
We said, 'If the wind's from over there
    There'll be rain tonight'.

                 .   .   .

Once pity we knew, and rage we knew,
    And pain we knew, too well,
As we stared and peered dizzily
    Through the gates of hell.

But now hell's gates are an old tale;
    Remote the anguish seems;
The guns are muffled and far away,
    Dreams within dreams.

And far and far are Flanders mud,
  And the pain of Picardy;
And the blood that runs there runs beyond
  The wide waste sea.

We are shut about by guarding walls:
  (We have built them lest we run
Mad from dreaming of naked fear
  And of black things done).

We are ringed all round by guarding walls,
  So high, they shut the view.
Not all the guns that shatter the world
  Can quite break through.

                .   .   .

Oh, guns of France, oh, guns of France,
  Be still, you crash in vain. . . .
Heavily up the south wind throb
  Dull dreams of pain, . . .

Be still, be still, south wind, lest your
  Blowing should bring the rain. . . .
We'll lie very quiet on Hurt Hill,
  And sleep once again.

Oh, we'll lie quite still, nor listen nor look,
  While the earth's bounds reel and shake,
Lest, battered too long, our walls and we
  Should break . . . should break. . . .

THE SHADOW
There was a Shadow on the moon; I saw it poise and tilt, and go
Its lonely way, and so I know that the blue velvet night will soon
Blaze loud and bright, as if the stars were crashing right into the
    town,
And tumbling streets and houses down, and smashing people like
    wine-jars. . . .

> *Fear wakes:*
> *What then?*
> *Strayed shadow of the Fear that breaks*
> *The world's young men.*

Bright fingers point all round the sky, they point and grope and
    cannot find.
(God's hand, you'd think, and he gone blind.) . . . The queer
    white faces twist and cry.
Last time they came they messed our square, and left it a hot
    rubbish-heap,
With people sunk in it so deep, you could not even hear them
    swear.

> *Fire blinds.*
> *What then?*
> *Pale shadow of the Pain that grinds*
> *The world's young men.*

The weak blood running down the street, oh, does it run like
    fire, like wine?
Are the spilt brains so keen, so fine, crushed limbs so swift, dead
    dreams so sweet?
There is a Plain where limbs and dreams and brains to set the
    world a-fire
Lie tossed in sodden heaps of mire. . . . Crash! Tonight's show
    begins, it seems.

> *Death . . . Well,*
> *What then?*
> *Rim of the shadow of the Hell*
> *Of the world's young men.*

Nina Macdonald

SING A SONG OF WAR-TIME

Sing a song of War-time,
Soldiers marching by,
Crowds of people standing,
Waving them 'Good-bye'.
When the crowds are over,
Home we go to tea,
Bread and margarine to eat,
War economy!

If I ask for cake, or
Jam of any sort,
Nurse says, 'What! in War-time?
Archie, cert'nly not!'
Life's not very funny
Now, for little boys,
Haven't any money,
Can't buy any toys.

Mummie does the house-work,
Can't get any maid,
Gone to make munitions,
'Cause they're better paid,
Nurse is always busy,
Never time to play,
Sewing shirts for soldiers,
Nearly ev'ry day.

Ev'ry body's doing
Something for the War,
Girls are doing things
They've never done before,
Go as 'bus conductors,
Drive a car or van,
All the world is topsy-turvy
Since the War began.

Florence Ripley Mastin

AT THE MOVIES

They swing across the screen in brave array,
   Long British columns grinding the dark grass.
Twelve months ago they marched into the grey
   Of battle; yet again behold them pass!

One lifts his dusty cap; his hair is bright;
   I meet his eyes, eager and young and bold.
The picture quivers into ghostly white;
   Then I remember, and my heart grows cold!

January, 1916

THE CENOTAPH

September 1919

Not yet will those measureless fields be green again
Where only yesterday the wild sweet blood of wonderful youth
    was shed;
There is a grave whose earth must hold too long, too deep a stain,
Though for ever over it we may speak as proudly as we may
    tread.
But here, where the watchers by lonely hearths from the thrust of
    an inward sword have more slowly bled,
We shall build the Cenotaph: Victory, winged, with Peace,
    winged too, at the column's head.
And over the stairway, at the foot – oh! here, leave desolate,
    passionate hands to spread
Violets, roses, and laurel, with the small, sweet, twinkling
    country things
Speaking so wistfully of other Springs,
From the little gardens of little places where son or sweetheart
    was born and bred.
In splendid sleep, with a thousand brothers
                To lovers – to mothers
                Here, too, lies he:
Under the purple, the green, the red,
It is all young life: it must break some women's hearts to see
Such a brave, gay coverlet to such a bed!
Only, when all is done and said,
God is not mocked and neither are the dead.
For this will stand in our Market-place –
                Who'll sell, who'll buy
                (Will you or I
Lie each to each with the better grace)?
While looking into every busy whore's and huckster's face
As they drive their bargains, is the Face
Of God: and some young, piteous, murdered face.

Charlotte Mew

MAY, 1915

    Let us remember Spring will come again
        To the scorched, blackened woods, where the
          wounded trees
   Wait with their old wise patience for the heavenly rain,
  Sure of the sky: sure of the sea to send its healing breeze,
     Sure of the sun. And even as to these
        Surely the Spring, when God shall please,
     Will come again like a divine surprise
To those who sit today with their great Dead, hands in their
  hands, eyes in their eyes,
At one with Love, at one with Grief: blind to the scattered things
  and changing skies.

JUNE, 1915

Who thinks of June's first rose today?
     Only some child, perhaps, with shining eyes and
       rough bright hair will reach it down
In a green sunny lane, to us almost as far away
   As are the fearless stars from these veiled lamps of town.
   What's little June to a great broken world with eyes gone
    dim
   From too much looking on the face of grief, the face of
    dread?
     Or what's the broken world to June and him
   Of the small eager hand, the shining eyes, the rough bright
    head?

Alice Meynell

'LORD, I OWE THEE A DEATH'
(Richard Hooker)

Man pays that debt with new munificence,
   Not piecemeal now, not slowly, by the old:
Not grudgingly, by the effaced thin pence,
   But greatly and in gold.

SUMMER IN ENGLAND, 1914

On London fell a clearer light;
   Caressing pencils of the sun
Defined the distances, the white
   Houses transfigured one by one,
The 'long, unlovely street' impearled.
O what a sky has walked the world!

Most happy year! And out of town
   The hay was prosperous, and the wheat;
The silken harvest climbed the down:
   Moon after moon was heavenly-sweet,
Stroking the bread within the sheaves,
Looking 'twixt apples and their leaves.

And while this rose made round her cup,
   The armies died convulsed. And when
This chaste young silver sun went up
   Softly, a thousand shattered men,
One wet corruption, heaped the plain,
After a league-long throb of pain.

Flower following tender flower; and birds,
   And berries; and benignant skies
Made thrive the serried flocks and herds. –
   Yonder are men shot through the eyes.
       Love, hide thy face
From man's unpardonable race.

.   .   .

Who said 'No man hath greater love than this,
　　To die to serve his friend'?
So these have loved us all unto the end.
　　Chide thou no more, O thou unsacrificed!
The soldier dying dies upon a kiss,
　　The very kiss of Christ.

HE WENT FOR A SOLDIER

He marched away with a blithe young score of him
  With the first volunteers,
Clear-eyed and clean and sound to the core of him,
  Blushing under the cheers.
They were fine, new flags that swung a-flying there,
Oh, the pretty girls he glimpsed a-crying there,
  Pelting him with pinks and with roses –
  Billy, the Soldier Boy!

Not very clear in the kind young heart of him
  What the fuss was about,
But the flowers and the flags seemed part of him –
  The music drowned his doubt.
It's a fine, brave sight they were a-coming there
To the gay, bold tune they kept a-drumming there,
  While the boasting fifes shrilled jauntily –
  Billy, the Soldier Boy!

Soon he is one with the blinding smoke of it –
  Volley and curse and groan:
Then he has done with the knightly joke of it –
  It's rending flesh and bone.
There are pain-crazed animals a-shrieking there
And a warm blood stench that is a-reeking there;
  He fights like a rat in a corner –
  Billy, the Soldier Boy!

There he lies now, like a ghoulish score of him,
  Left on the field for dead:
The ground all around is smeared with the gore of him –
  Even the leaves are red.
The Thing that was Billy lies a-dying there,
Writhing and a-twisting and a-crying there;
  A sickening sun grins down on him –
  Billy, the Soldier Boy!

Still not quite clear in the poor, wrung heart of him
  What the fuss was about,

See where he lies – or a ghastly part of him –
    While life is oozing out:
There are loathsome things he sees a-crawling there;
There are hoarse-voiced crows he hears a-calling there,
    Eager for the foul feast spread for them –
    Billy, the Soldier Boy!

How much longer, O Lord, shall we bear it all?
    How many more red years?
Story it and glory it and share it all,
    In seas of blood and tears?
They are braggart attitudes we've worn so long;
They are tinsel platitudes we've sworn so long –
    We who have turned the Devil's Grindstone,
    Borne with the hell called War!

ON THE PORCH

As I lie roofed in, screened in,
From the pattering rain,
The summer rain –
As I lie
Snug and dry,
And hear the birds complain:

Oh, billow on billow,
Oh, roar on roar,
Over me wash
The seas of war.
Over me – down – down –
Lunges and plunges
The huge gun with its one blind eye,
The armoured train,
And, swooping out of the sky,
The aeroplane.
Down – down –
The army proudly swinging
Under gay flags,
The glorious dead heaped up like rags,
A church with bronze bells ringing,
A city all towers,
Gardens of lovers and flowers,
The round world swinging
In the light of the sun:
All broken, undone,
All down – under
Black surges of thunder . . .

Oh, billow on billow
Oh, roar on roar,
Over me wash
The seas of war . . .

As I lie roofed in, screened in,
From the pattering rain,

Harriet Monroe

The summer rain –
As I lie
Snug and dry,
And hear the birds complain.

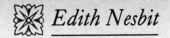

THE FIELDS OF FLANDERS

Last year the fields were all glad and gay
With silver daisies and silver may;
There were kingcups gold by the river's edge
And primrose stars under every hedge.

This year the fields are trampled and brown,
The hedges are broken and beaten down,
And where the primroses used to grow
Are little black crosses set in a row.

And the flower of hopes, and the flowers of dreams,
The noble, fruitful, beautiful schemes,
The tree of life with its fruit and bud,
Are trampled down in the mud and the blood.

The changing seasons will bring again
The magic of Spring to our wood and plain:
Though the Spring be so green as never was seen
The crosses will still be black in the green.

The God of battles shall judge the foe
Who trampled our country and laid her low. . . .
God! hold our hands on the reckoning day,
Lest all we owe them we should repay.

1915

SPRING IN WAR-TIME

Now the sprinkled blackthorn snow
   Lies along the lovers' lane
Where last year we used to go –
   Where we shall not go again.

In the hedge the buds are new,
   By our wood the violets peer –
Just like last year's violets, too,
   But they have no scent this year.

Edith Nesbit

Every bird has heart to sing
   Of its nest, warmed by its breast;
We had heart to sing last spring,
   But we never built our nest.

Presently red roses blown
   Will make all the garden gay. . . .
Not yet have the daisies grown
   On your clay.

   1916

Eileen Newton

LAST LEAVE
(1918)
Let us forget tomorrow! For tonight
At least, with curtains drawn, and driftwood piled
On our own hearthstone, we may rest, and see
The firelight flickering on familiar walls.
(How the blue flames leap when an ember falls!)
Peace, and content, and soul-security –
These are within. Without, the waste is wild
With storm-clouds sweeping by in furious flight,
And ceaseless beating of autumnal rain
Upon our window pane.

The dusk grows deeper now, the flames are low:
We do not heed the shadows, you and I,
Nor fear the grey wings of encroaching gloom,
So softly they enfold us. One last gleam
Flashes and flits, elusive as a dream,
And then dies out upon the darkened room.
So, even so, our earthly fires must die;
Yet, in our hearts, love's flame shall leap and glow
When this dear night, with all it means to me,
Is but a memory!

REVISION
(For November 11th)
In those two silent moments, when we stand
To let the surging tide of memory fill
The mind's deep caverns with its mingled flood
Of joys and griefs, I shall not think again,
As I was wont, of the untimely slain,
Of poppies dipped and dyed in human blood,
Of the rude cross upon the ravaged hill,
And all the strife which scarred that lovely land.

Eileen Newton

My thoughts shall seek, instead, a hallowed place –
The little, leafy wood where you and I
Spent the last hour together, while the breeze
Lulled every nodding daffodil to rest;
And from the flaming ramparts of the west
Shone bars of gold between black stems of trees,
Till dusk crept softly down the April sky,
And Hesperus trembled in the sapphire space.

Remembering this, my heart, at length set free
From gyves of hate, its bitter passion shed,
May hear once more the low, caressing call
That so entranced it, seven sad years ago.
Then, in those poignant moments, I shall know
That pain and parting matter not at all,
Because your soul, long-risen from the dead,
Is crowned by love's immortal constancy.

�֎ *Eleanour Norton*

IN A RESTAURANT, 1917

Encircled by the traffic's roar
Midst music and the blaze of light,
The battle-jaded khaki knights
Throng, sleek and civilised once more.

Oh, one there was who, long ago
(Three centuries or is it years?)
Adored the splendour and the tears
Of London Ebb – of London Flow.

Oh, one whose very presence gave
The common air an added grace,
Now in our hearts an empty place
And far in France an unmarked grave.

AMBULANCE TRAIN 30

A.T. 30 lies in the siding.
Above her cold grey clouds lie, silver-long as she.
Like a great battleship that never saw defeat
She dreams: while the pale day dies down
Behind the harbour town,
Beautiful, complete
And unimpassioned as the long grey sea.

A.T. 30 lies in the siding.
Gone are her red crosses – the sick that were her own.
Like a great battleship that never saw defeat
She waits, while the pale day dies down
Behind the harbour town,
Beautiful, complete. . . .
And the Occupying Army boards her for Cologne.

   May 6, 1919

BRUSSELS, 1919

Wide are the streets, and driven clean
With slanting rain. Behind tall gates
The lilac trees shoot silver green.
The boulevards sing with traffic. Still
The arches triumph on each hill.
And the victorious city waits
But for her soldiers' homecoming.

The shops are bright in fresh array.
The tramcars ring and jangle by
Crowded with soldiers. Every day
Brings home to her more exiled sons –
Dawns grey upon more captured guns –
And just outside the city lie
Her forests, warm with welcoming. . . .

A mile or two outside the town
The silent forests stand; that spread

Down where the road has faded brown
And the pale leaves fall silver red,
Thick underfoot in rise and swell
Damp with old rains and sweet to smell,
Red underfoot, red overhead.

The road is white beneath the moon.
Go on until the dawn is new,
And you may meet the strange dragoon
And he may stop to ride with you.
(His men have faces pale as smoke,
But understand an English joke
Upon the road to Waterloo.)

May O'Rourke

THE MINORITY: 1917

She curls her darkened lashes; manicures
Her scented hands; rubs cream where by and by
The tell-tale lines will gather. –
                                        She is yours,
O Dead! who went to die

To save her light blue eyes from dreadful scenes,
To keep her dainty feet from broken ways,
Her youth from Hell – now see her as she preens
Bright thro' the weary days,

Tinkling her silly mirth against the dread
Calm of those lives who listen for dear feet
That will not come again.
                            – Ah! fool! you tread
No mere commercial street,

But ground made consecrate by their spilt lives
Who stood but yesterday where now you stand
And died; or grope in darkness; fret in gyves,
Or lack their good right hand;

Or stare with dark and witless eyes that brood
Dumbly, upon the panic of an hour
When all the world was red.
                            – And *you* are hued
Gay, as a painted flower,
Filling our days with foolishness and noise
And wooing Love with all your careful arts,
Forgetting quite the thousand, thousand boys
Who gave you their pierced hearts!

Emily Orr

A RECRUIT FROM THE SLUMS

'What has your country done for you,
    Child of a city slum,
That you should answer her ringing call
To man the gap and keep the wall
And hold the field though a thousand fall
    And help be slow to come?

'What has your country given to you,
    Her poor relation and friend?'
'Oh, a fight like death for your board and keep,
And some pitiful silver coins per week
    And the thought of the "house" at the end.'

'What can your country ask from you,
    Dregs of the British race?'
'She gave us little, she taught us less,
And why we were born we could hardly guess
Till we felt the surge of battle press
    And looked the foe in the face.'

'Greater love hath no man than this
    That a man should die for his friend.'
'We thought life cruel, and England cold;
But our bones were made from the English mould,
And when all is said, she's our mother old
    And we creep to her breast at the end.'

Jessie Pope

THE CALL

Who's for the trench –
   Are you, my laddie?
Who'll follow French –
   Will you, my laddie?
Who's fretting to begin,
Who's going out to win?
And who wants to save his skin –
   Do you, my laddie?

Who's for the khaki suit –
   Are you, my laddie?
Who longs to charge and shoot –
   Do you, my laddie?
Who's keen on getting fit,
Who means to show his grit,
And who'd rather wait a bit –
   Would you, my laddie?

Who'll earn the Empire's thanks –
   Will you, my laddie?
Who'll swell the victor's ranks –
   Will you, my laddie?
When that procession comes,
Banners and rolling drums –
Who'll stand and bite his thumbs –
   Will you, my laddie?

THE NUT'S BIRTHDAY

When Gilbert's birthday came *last* spring,
   Oh! how our brains we racked
To try and find a single thing
   Our languid dear one lacked;
For, since he nestled at his ease
   Upon the lap of Plenty,
Stock birthday presents failed to please
   The Nut of two and twenty.

And so we bought, to suit his taste –
   Refined and dilettante –
Some ormolu, grotesquely chased;
   A little bronze Bacchante;
A flagon of the Stuarts' reign;
   A 'Corot' to content him.
Well, now his birthday's come again,
   And *this* is what we sent him:

Some candles and a bar of soap,
   Cakes, peppermints and matches,
A pot of jam, some thread (like rope)
   For stitching khaki patches.
These gifts, our soldier writes to say,
   Have brought him untold riches
To celebrate his natal day
   In hard-won Flanders' ditches.

SOCKS

Shining pins that dart and click
   In the fireside's sheltered peace
Check the thoughts that cluster thick –
   20 plain and then decrease.

He was brave – well, so was I –
   Keen and merry, but his lip
Quivered when he said good-bye –
   Purl the seam-stitch, purl and slip.

Never used to living rough,
   Lots of things he'd got to learn;
Wonder if he's warm enough –
   Knit 2, catch 2, knit 1, turn.

Hark! The paper-boys again!
   Wish that shout could be suppressed;
Keeps one always on the strain –
   Knit off 9, and slip the rest.

Wonder if he's fighting now,
    What he's done an' where he's been;
He'll come out on top, somehow –
    Slip 1, knit 2, purl 14.

WAR GIRLS

There's the girl who clips your ticket for the train,
    And the girl who speeds the lift from floor to floor,
There's the girl who does a milk-round in the rain,
    And the girl who calls for orders at your door.
            Strong, sensible, and fit,
            They're out to show their grit,
    And tackle jobs with energy and knack.
            No longer caged and penned up,
            They're going to keep their end up
Till the khaki soldier boys come marching back.

There's the motor girl who drives a heavy van,
    There's the butcher girl who brings your joint of meat,
There's the girl who cries 'All fares, please!' like a man,
    And the girl who whistles taxis up the street.
            Beneath each uniform
            Beats a heart that's soft and warm,
    Though of canny mother-wit they show no lack;
            But a solemn statement this is,
            They've no time for love and kisses
Till the khaki soldier boys come marching back.

Inez Quilter (Aged 11 years)

'SALL'
(In Aid of the Wounded Horses)

I'm none of yer London gentry,
None o' yer Hyde Park swells,
But I'm only a farmer's plough horse
And I'se born among hills and fells.

Yer mus'n't expect no graces
For yer won't get 'em from me,
I'se made as nature intended
An' I'm jus' plain Sall, d'ye see.

You've not seen me in the Row yet
An' yer won't, if yer try so 'ard,
I'm not a show 'orse yer forget
But I'm Sall, plain Sall, and Sall goes 'ard!

Dorothy Una Ratcliffe

REMEMBRANCE DAY IN THE DALES

It's a fine kind thought! And yet – I know
The Abbey's not where our Jack should lie,
With his sturdy love of a rolling sky;
        As a tiny child
He loved a sea that was grand and wild.
        God knows best!
Near-by the sea our Jack should rest.

And Willie – Willie our youngest born –
I fear that he might be lonesome, laid
Where the echoing, deep-voiced prayers are said, –
And yet the deep-voiced praying words
Reach God's heart too with the hymns of the birds.
        In His keep
On the edge of a wood our Will should sleep.
        God knows best!
But the years are long since the lads went west.

92

THE CENOTAPH

The man in the Trilby hat has furtively shifted it;
The man with the clay pipe has pushed his fists deeper into his
    pockets;
Beparcelled women are straining their necks
To stare.
Through the spattered windows of the omnibus
We see,
Dumb beneath the rain,
Marshalled by careful policemen,
Four behind four,
The relatives of dead heroes,
Clutching damp wreaths.
Within the omnibus there is silence
But for a sniff.
Then a plump woman speaks,
Softly, unquerulously:
'I wouldn't', she says,
'I wouldn't stand in a queue to have my feelings harrowed,
Not my*self*, I wouldn't.'
The omnibus swerves to the pavement,
And the plump woman
Prepares for equable departure.
'But there,' she adds unbitterly,
'I often think it wouldn't do
For us all to be alike.
There's some as can't,
But then, again,
There's some, you see,
As can.'
Beautiful,
Plump woman,
(Plump of mind as well as of body)
Beautiful is your tolerance
Of human idiosyncrasy.
When my impatient feet would tap in irritation,
When my breath would break out in abuse,

When my scornful lips would frame themselves
(At the vices,
Or at the virtues,
Of my neighbours)
Into a sneer only half pitiful,
May I remember you
And murmur with serenity,
Without intensity,
Without virulence,
'I wouldn't,
Not myself,
But then, again,
There's some, you see,
As can'.

Margaret Sackville

A MEMORY

There was no sound at all, no crying in the village,
    Nothing you would count as sound, that is, after the shells;
Only behind a wall the low sobbing of women,
    The creaking of a door, a lost dog – nothing else.

Silence which might be felt, no pity in the silence,
    Horrible, soft like blood, down all the blood-stained ways;
In the middle of the street two corpses lie unburied,
    And a bayoneted woman stares in the market-place.

Humble and ruined folk – for these no pride of conquest,
    Their only prayer: 'O! Lord, give us our daily bread!'
Not by the battle fires, the shrapnel are we haunted;
    Who shall deliver us from the memory of these dead?

SACRAMENT

Before the Altar of the world in flower,
    Upon whose steps thy creatures kneel in line,
We do beseech Thee in this wild Spring hour,
    Grant us, O Lord, thy wine. But not this wine.

Helpless, we, praying by Thy shimmering seas,
    Beside Thy fields, whence all the world is fed,
Thy little children clinging about Thy knees,
    Cry: 'Grant us, Lord, Thy bread!' But not this bread.

This wine of awful sacrifice outpoured;
    This bread of life – of human lives. The Press
Is overflowing, the Wine-Press of the Lord! . . .
    Yet doth he tread the foaming grapes no less.

These stricken lands! The green time of the year
    Has found them wasted by a purple flood,
Sodden and wasted everywhere, everywhere; –
    Not all our tears may cleanse them from that blood.

The earth is all too narrow for our dead,
    So many and each a child of ours – and Thine
This flesh (our flesh) crumbled away like bread,
    This blood (our blood) poured out like wine, like wine.

Aimee Byng Scott

JULY 1ST, 1916

                    A soft grey mist,
Poppies flamed brilliant where the woodlands bend
Or straggling in amongst the ripening corn,
                    Green grass dew kist;
While distantly a lark's pure notes ascend,
                    Greeting the morn.

                    A shuddering night;
Flames, not of poppies, cleave the quivering air,
The corn is razed, the twisted trees are dead;
                    War in his might
Has passed; Nature lies prostrate there
                    Stunned by his tread.

May Sinclair

FIELD AMBULANCE IN RETREAT
Via Dolorosa, Via Sacra

I

A straight flagged road, laid on the rough earth,
A causeway of stone from beautiful city to city,
Between the tall trees, the slender, delicate trees,
Through the flat green land, by plots of flowers, by black canals
    thick with heat.

II

The road-makers made it well
Of fine stone, strong for the feet of the oxen and of the great
    Flemish horses,
And for the high wagons piled with corn from the harvest.
And the labourers are few;
They and their quiet oxen stand aside and wait
By the long road loud with the passing of the guns, the rush of
    armoured cars, and the tramp of an army on the march
    forward to battle;
And, where the piled corn-wagons went, our dripping
    Ambulance carries home
Its red and white harvest from the fields.

III

The straight flagged road breaks into dust, into a thin white
    cloud,
About the feet of a regiment driven back league by league,
Rifles at trail, and standards wrapped in black funeral cloths.
Unhasting, proud in retreat,
They smile as the Red Cross Ambulance rushes by.
(You know nothing of beauty and of desolation who have not seen
That smile of an army in retreat.)
They go: and our shining, beckoning danger goes with them,
And our joy in the harvests that we gathered in at nightfall in the
    fields;
And like an unloved hand laid on a beating heart
Our safety weighs us down.

Safety hard and strange; stranger and yet more hard
As, league after dying league, the beautiful, desolate Land
Falls back from the intolerable speed of an Ambulance in retreat
On the sacred, dolorous Way.

Edith Sitwell

THE DANCERS
(During a Great Battle, 1916)

The floors are slippery with blood:
The world gyrates too. God is good
That while His wind blows out the light
For those who hourly die for us –
We still can dance, each night.

The music has grown numb with death –
But we will suck their dying breath,
The whispered name they breathed to chance,
To swell our music, make it loud
That we may dance, – may dance.

We are the dull blind carrion-fly
That dance and batten. Though God die
Mad from the horror of the light –
The light is mad, too, flecked with blood, –
We dance, we dance, each night.

THE CONVALESCENT

We've billards, bowls an' tennis courts, we've teas an' motor-
   rides;
We've concerts nearly every night, an' 'eaps o' things besides;
We've all the best of everything as much as we can eat –
But my 'eart – my 'eart's at 'ome in 'Enry Street.

I'm askin' Sister every day when I'll be fit to go;
'We must 'ave used you bad' (she says) 'you want to leave us so';
I says, 'I beg your pardon, Nurse, the place is 'ard to beat,
But my 'eart – my 'eart's at 'ome in 'Enry Street.'

The sheffoneer we saved to buy, the clock upon the wall,
The pictures an' the almanac, the china dogs an' all,
I've thought about it many a time, my little 'ome complete,
When in Flanders, far away from 'Enry Street.

It's 'elped me through the toughest times – an' some was middlin'
   tough –
The 'ardest march was not so 'ard, the roughest not so rough;
It's 'elped me keep my pecker up in victory an' defeat,
Just to think about my 'ome in 'Enry Street.

There's several things I'd like to 'ave which 'ere I never see,
I'd like some chipped potatoes an' a kipper to my tea;
But most of all I'd like to feel the stones beneath my feet
Of the road that takes me 'ome to 'Enry Street.

They'll 'ave a little flag 'ung out – they'll 'ave the parlour gay
With crinkled paper all about, the same as Christmas Day,
An' out of all the neighbours' doors the 'eads 'll pop to greet
Me comin' wounded 'ome to 'Enry Street.

My missis – well, she'll cry a bit, an' laugh a bit between;
My kids 'll climb upon my knees – there's one I've never seen;
An' of all the days which I 'ave known there won't be one so sweet
As the one when I go 'ome to 'Enry Street.

Marie Carmichael Stopes

NIGHT ON THE SHORE
Northumberland. August 6th, 1914

A dusky owl in velvet moth-like flight,
With feathers spread on non-resistant air,
Wheels on its silent wings, brushing my cheek.
The circles of its course are interlaced
By chuckling seagull-flocks, whose wide white wings
Sweep down to settle on the bare-ribbed sand
Left rich with treasure by the distant tide.
The owl gyrates, a part of the soft air,
Then upright, solemn, on my lowly tent
Perches beside me with his eyes intent
As though upon Minerva's shoulder. He
And I together watch the waves of cloud
Which slowly break and ripple o'er the moon,
Silvering celestial foam from their frayed edge.
The dim ethereal curve of the wide sand
Is flecked with hard black shadows, heightening
The fairy mountains left there in their play
By little weary waves which slid away
To slumber, cradled by the green-haired rocks.
Through the still water star-reflections deck
The red anemones with diadems.
This cosmic peace the owl and I have shared
For a whole moon of deep experience.

. . .

Tonight the moonbeams break on bayonets
Sharpened and gleaming in hot eager hands.
Tonight the swift low rush of battleships
Throbs up and down the bay, waking the waves.
Tonight my sleep is challenged in my tent
By martial voices backed by gleaming steel.
Tonight young men from cities meet the stars
When scanning the horizon for their foes.
Tonight there thrills all round our peaceful shores

The pulsing chain of men who wait on war.
And War, insensate, drills its brutal way
Through quivering hearts and sets men's pulses mad
With burning rage to rend the strong and fair,
If only they were born on other shores.

.   .   .

And yet – tonight – our young men from the town
Sleep under the high arches of the stars
And keep their watch in crystal, moonlit air,
Perforce within God's presence, too.

Muriel Stuart

FORGOTTEN DEAD, I SALUTE YOU

Dawn has flashed up the startled skies,
Night has gone out beneath the hill
Many sweet times; before our eyes
Dawn makes and unmakes about us still
The magic that we call the rose.
The gentle history of the rain
Has been unfolded, traced and lost
By the sharp finger-tips of frost;
Birds in the hawthorn build again;
The hare makes soft her secret house;
The wind at tourney comes and goes,
Spurring the green, unharnessed boughs;
The moon has waxed fierce and waned dim:
He knew the beauty of all those
Last year, and who remembers him?

Love sometimes walks the waters still,
Laughter throws back her radiant head;
Utterly beauty is not gone,
And wonder is not wholly dead.
The starry, mortal world rolls on;
Between sweet sounds and silences,
With new, strange wines her beakers brim:
He lost his heritage with these
Last year, and who remembers him?

None remember him: he lies
In earth of some strange-sounding place,
Nameless beneath the nameless skies,
The wind his only chant, the rain
The only tears upon his face;
Far and forgotten utterly
By living man. Yet such as he
Have made it possible and sure
For other lives to have, to be;
For men to sleep content, secure.
Lip touches lip and eyes meet eyes

Because his heart beats not again:
His rotting, fruitless body lies
That sons may grow from other men.

He gave, as Christ, the life he had –
The only life desired or known;
The great, sad sacrifice was made
For strangers; this forgotten dead
Went out into the night alone.
There was his body broken for you,
There was his blood divinely shed
That in the earth lie lost and dim.
Eat, drink, and often as you do,
For whom he died, remember him.

Millicent Sutherland

ONE NIGHT

I walked into a moon of gold last night,
Across grey sands she seemed to shine so bright.

Wide, wide the sands until I met the sea,
Cradle of moons, yet searchlights followed me.

I asked the moon if creeping round the Zones
She had seen good, or only poor things' bones.

'Pale faces I have seen, unconscious men
Bereft of struggling horror now and then.

'And sinking ships I see, and floating mines,
And cries I hear, "O God", and choking whines.

'But later when the stars shine on the wave
And give more light, I know the dead die brave.

'Passing so quickly from the things that count,
Count to all mortal thoughts, to find the Fount,

'Where angels pour elixir into bowls,
Drink, not for broken hearts, but thirsty souls.'

'And what on shore?' I asked, 'the great Divide
Where rivers run, and trenches side by side?'

'There,' the moon said, 'the snow was on the ground
And the frost pinched me as I beamed around.

'Red pools of gore, and ghastly shadows lay
In deep dug corners, so I sank away.

'Let misty cloudlets sweep across my face
To hide the earth, and give me heart of grace.

'Sudden the air seemed filled with eager breath
Of great Adventurers, released from death,

'And shaking blood from out their eyes and hair
Shouting for further knowledge here and there.

106

'I lighted these across the treacherous Path
To reach the garden of Life's aftermath.

'And as they sped in troops the great guns boomed,
With flashes lightning swift, and dark hordes loomed,

'And phantom shapes of patient warrior bands –
Then more snow fell and shrouded all the lands.'

.   .

Now pondering from the moon I turned again,
Over the sands, back to our House of Pain.

British Hospital,
Malo, Dunkirk, France

✳ *C.A.L.T.*

Y.M.C.A.

Oh Monday night's the night for me!
On happy Mondays, after tea,
We canteen helpers drive to ——
(To name the camp would be too rash,
For Zepps our whereabouts might learn
And bombs come dropping in the urn).

We stand and wait behind the bar:
You've no idea how smart we are
At serving Horlick's, tea and 'pop'
To thirsty Tommies, and our shop
Sells cakes, and chocolate and smokes.
We're up to all the little jokes:
And, asked for 'coffin-nails' by wags,
Produce 'Wild Woodbines', well-loved fags.

Some linger for a friendly chat,
Some call me 'Mother' – Think of that!
And often, at the magic word,
My vision grows a little blurred –
The crowd in khaki disappears,
I see them through a mist of years:
I see them in a thousand prams –
A thousand mothers' little lambs . . .

'One bar nut-milk, two scones and teas?
That's fivepence – no; not money please,
Get tickets near the door – for soap,
For note-paper and envelope
Turn to the left' . . . Ah! Tommy dear,
I often wonder if you hear
Me murmur 'Thank you', as I take
Your tickets for the tea and cake,
And tear them up – or understand
I'd like to shake your grimy hand?

Two simple words are all I say,
I've saved them up for many a day –

108

Just 'thank you', but they mean a lot!
Accept them, for they're all I've got
To tell my gratitude, they come
Straight from my heart. On Monday, some
Five hundred times I say them o'er,
And wish it were five hundred more!

.   .   .

And when the Camp is wrapped in sleep,
Ere wearily to bed I creep,
Oh Tommy Atkins! brave and true –
I humbly thank my God for you.

August, 1915

Sara Teasdale

SPRING IN WAR-TIME

I feel the Spring far off, far off,
    The faint far scent of bud and leaf —
Oh how can Spring take heart to come
    To a world in grief,
        Deep grief?

The sun turns north, the days grow long,
    Later the evening star grows bright —
How can the daylight linger on
    For men to fight,
        Still fight?

The grass is waking in the ground,
    Soon it will rise and blow in waves —
How can it have the heart to sway
    Over the graves,
        New graves?

Under the boughs where lovers walked
    The apple-blooms will shed their breath —
But what of all the lovers now
    Parted by death,
        Grey Death?

'THERE WILL COME SOFT RAINS'

There will come soft rains and the smell of the ground,
And swallows calling with their shimmering sound;

And frogs in the pools singing at night,
And wild-plum trees in tremulous white;

Robins will wear their feathery fire
Whistling their whims on a low fence-wire;

And not one will know of the war, not one
Will care at last when it is done.

Not one would mind, neither bird nor tree,
If mankind perished utterly;

And Spring herself, when she woke at dawn,
Would scarcely know that we were gone.

IN TIME OF WAR

I dreamed (God pity babes at play)
   How I should love past all romance,
And how to him beloved should say,
   As heroes' women say, perchance,
     When the deep drums awake –
     'Go forth: do gloriously for my dear sake.'

But now I render, blind with fear,
   No lover made of dreams, but You,
O You – so commonplace, so dear,
   So knit with all I am or do!
     Now, braver thought I lack:
     Only God bring you back – God bring you back!

Aelfrida Tillyard

INVITATION AU FESTIN

Oh come and live with me, my love,
    And share my war-time dinner.
Who eats the least at this our feast,
    Shall make John Bull the winner.

Here is a plate of cabbage soup,
    With caterpillars in.
How good they taste! (Avoid all waste,
    If you the war would win.)

Now, will you have a minnow, love,
    Or half an inch of eel?
A stickleback, a slice of jack,
    Shall grace our festive meal.

We've no unpatriotic joint,
    No sugar and no bread.
Eat nothing sweet, no rolls, no meat,
    The Food Controller said.

But would you like some sparrow pie,
    To counteract the eel?
A slice of swede is what you need,
    And please don't leave the peel.

But there's dessert for you, my love,
    Some glucose stewed with sloes.
And now good-night – your dreams be bright!
    (Perhaps they will – who knows?)

A LETTER FROM EALING BROADWAY STATION
(From E.M.W.T.)

'Night. Fog. Tall through the murky gloom
The coloured lights of signals loom,
And underneath my boot I feel
The long recumbent lines of steel.

Aelfrida Tillyard

As up and down the beat I tramp
My face and hair are wet with damp;
My hands are cold – that's but a trifle –
And I must mind the sentry's rifle.
'Twould be a foolish way to die,
Mistaken for a German spy!
Hardest of all is just to keep
Open my eyelids drugged with sleep.

Stand back! With loud metallic crash
And lighted windows all a-flash
The train to Bristol past me booms.

I wonder who has got my rooms!
I like to think that Frank is there,
And Willie in the basket-chair,
While Ernest, with his guileless looks,
Is making havoc in my books.
The smoke-rings rise, and we discuss
Friendship, and What Life Means to Us,
What is it that the kitchens lack,
And where we'll take our tramp next vac.

Those girls at Newnham whom I taught
I'll spare them each a friendly thought . . .

An hour to dawn! I'd better keep
Moving, or I shall fall asleep.

I've had before my eyes these days
The fires of Antwerp all ablaze.
(The startled women scream and weep;
Only the dead have time to sleep.)
I'd like to feel that I was helping
To send the German curs a-yelping.
Well, if I serve the Belgian nation
By guarding Ealing Broadway station,
I'll guard it gladly, never fear.

Sister, good-night; the dawn is here.'

Cambridge, October 11, 1914

114

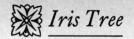

Iris Tree

Poem untitled

Of all who died in silence far away
Where sympathy was busy with other things,
Busy with worlds, inventing how to slay,
Troubled with rights and wrongs and governments and kings.

The little dead who knew so large a love,
Whose lives were sweet unto themselves a shepherding
Of hopes, ambitions, wonders in a drove
Over the hills of time, that now are graves for burying.

Of all the tenderness that flowed to them,
A milky way streaming from out their mother's breast,
Stars were they to her night, and she the stem
From which they flowered – now barren and left unblessed.

Of all the sparkling kisses that they gave
Spangling a secret radiance on adoring hands,
Now stifled in the darkness of a grave
With kiss of loneliness and death's embracing bands.

No more! – And we, the mourners, dare not wear
The black that folds our hearts in secrecy of pain,
But must don purple and bright standards bear,
Vermilion of our honour, a bloody train.

We dare not weep who must be brave in battle –
'Another death – another day – another inch of land –
The dead are cheering and the ghost drums rattle' . . .
The dead are deaf and dumb and cannot understand. . . .

Of all who died in darkness far away
Nothing is left of them but LOVE, who triumphs now,
His arms held crosswise to the budding day,
The passion-red roses clustering his brow.

1917

Poem untitled

And afterwards, when honour has made good,
And all you think you fight for shall take place,
A late rejoicing to a crippled race;
The bulldog's teeth relax and snap for food,
The eagles fly to their forsaken brood,
Within the ravaged nest. When no disgrace
Shall spread a blush across the haggard face
Of anxious Pride, already flushed with blood.

In victory will you have conquered Hate,
And stuck old Folly with a bayonet
And battered down the hideous prison gate?
Or will the fatted gods be gloried yet,
Glutted with gold and dust and empty state,
The incense of our anguish and our sweat?

1917

THE HOSPITAL VISITOR

When yesterday I went to see my friends –
  (Watching their patient faces in a row
I want to give each boy a D.S.O.)
When yesterday I went to see my friends
With cigarettes, and foolish odds and ends,
  (Knowing they understand how well I know
That nothing I can do may make amends,
  But that I must not grieve, or tell them so),
A pale-faced Iniskilling, just eighteen,
  Who'd fought two years; with eyes a little dim
Smiled up and showed me, there behind the screen
  On the humped bandage that replaced a limb,
How someone left him, where the leg had been
  A tiny green glass pig to comfort him.

These are the men who've learned to laugh at pain.
  And if their lips have quivered when they spoke,
They've said brave words, or tried to make a joke.
Said it's not worse than trenches in the rain,
Or pools of water on a chalky plain,
  Or bitter cold from which you stiffly woke,
Or deep wet mud that left you hardly sane,
  Or the tense wait for 'Fritz's master stroke'.
You seldom hear them talk of their 'bad luck',
  And suffering has not spoiled their ready wit.
And oh! you'd hardly doubt their fighting pluck
  When each new operation shows their grit,
Who never brag of blows for England struck,
  But only yearn to 'get about a bit'.

THE BROKEN SOLDIER

The broken soldier sings and whistles day to dark;
    He's but the remnant of a man, maimed and half-blind,
But the soul they could not harm goes singing like the lark,
    Like the incarnate Joy that will not be confined.

The Lady at the Hall has given him a light task,
    He works in the gardens as busy as a bee;
One hand is but a stump and his face a pitted mask;
    The gay soul goes singing like a bird set free.

Whistling and singing like a linnet on wings;
    The others stop to listen, leaning on the spade,
Whole men and comely, they fret at little things.
    The soul of him's singing like a thrush in a glade.

Hither and thither, hopping, like Robin on the grass,
    The soul in the broken man is beautiful and brave;
And while he weeds the pansies and the bright hours pass,
    The bird caught in the cage whistles its joyous stave.

A GIRL'S SONG

The Meuse and Marne have little waves;
    The slender poplars o'er them lean.
One day they will forget the graves
    That give the grass its living green.

Some brown French girl the rose will wear
    That springs above his comely head;
Will twine it in her russet hair,
    Nor wonder why it is so red.

His blood is in the rose's veins,
    His hair is in the yellow corn.
My grief is in the weeping rains
    And in the keening wind forlorn.

Flow softly, softly, Marne and Meuse;
 Tread lightly all ye browsing sheep;
Fall tenderly, O silver dews,
 For here my dear Love lies asleep.

The earth is on his sealèd eyes,
 The beauty marred that was my pride;
Would I were lying where he lies,
 And sleeping sweetly by his side!

The Spring will come by Meuse and Marne,
 The birds be blithesome in the tree.
I heap the stones to make his cairn
 Where many sleep as sound as he.

JOINING THE COLOURS
(West Kents, Dublin, August 1914)

There they go marching all in step so gay!
 Smooth-cheeked and golden, food for shells and guns.
Blithely they go as to a wedding day,
 The mothers' sons.

The drab street stares to see them row on row
 On the high tram-tops, singing like the lark.
Too careless-gay for courage, singing they go
 Into the dark.

With tin whistles, mouth-organs, any noise,
 They pipe the way to glory and the grave;
Foolish and young, the gay and golden boys
 Love cannot save.

High heart! High courage! The poor girls they kissed
 Run with them: they shall kiss no more, alas!
Out of the mist they stepped – into the mist
 Singing they pass.

Viviane Verne

KENSINGTON GARDENS
(1915)

Dappling shadows on the summer grass,
    Vernal rivalry among the trees;
Lovers smiling coyly as they pass,
    Sparrows laughing in the summer breeze.

Children playing by the placid lake,
    Coaxing ducks, with greedy eyes;
Sunlight gilding ripplelets that break
    Where they struggle for a prize.

Jealous dogs that 'do delight'
    In frantic grappling for a stick,
Racing back with 'bark and bite',
    To yield a trophy quite historic.

Lonely ladies dreaming in bath-chairs,
    Old men taking sun baths on the seats,
Nurses softly talking in prim pairs,
    Telling of their soldier lovers' feats.

Medall'd patrols keeping austere guard
    Over radiant rose and ever-greens,
Gold-flecked finery and velvet sward,
    And the quiet garden of dead queens.

    Fleecy clouds in limpid blue,
        Smiling down with tender mien;
    Life seems simple, honest, true,
        In this simple open scene.

    Who would think that vault benign
        God's last area free from vice,
    Initiates the aerial mine,
        With babes below as sacrifice.

    Sitting here on summer morn,
        With the birds and babes at play,
    Who could dream that sky was torn
        Yesternight – with hellish spray.

120

It is strange that Nature's lurement
    Waits – unclaimed – for our retrievement,
While men war in false endurement
    Deeming this life's great achievement.

Alberta Vickridge

IN A V.A.D. PANTRY

Pots in piles of blue and white,
Old in service, cracked and chipped –
While the bare-armed girls tonight
Rinse and dry, with trivial-lipped
Mirth, and jests, and giggling chatter,
In this maze of curls and clatter
Is there no one sees in you
More than common white and blue?

When the potter trimmed your clay's
Sodden mass to his desire –
Washed you in the viscid glaze
That is clarified by fire –
When he sold your sort in lots,
Reckoning such as common pots –
Did he not at times foresee
Sorrow in your destiny?

Lips of fever, parched for drink
From this vessel seek relief
Ah, so often, that I think
Many a sad Last Supper's grief
Haunts it still – that they who died,
In man's quarrel crucified,
Shed a nimbus strange and pale
Round about this humble Grail.

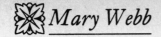 *Mary Webb*

AUTUMN, 1914

The scarlet-jewelled ashtree sighed – 'He cometh,
For whom no wine is poured and no bee hummeth.'

> The huddled bean-sheaves under the moon,
> Like black tents, will be vanished soon.
> So fast the days draw in and are over,
> So early the bees are gone from the clover –
> Today, tomorrow –
> And nights are dark, and as cold as sorrow.

> He's gone, her man, so good with his hands
> In the harvest field and the lambing shed.
> Straight ran his share in the deep ploughlands –
> And now he marches among the dead.

The ash let fall her gems, and moaned – 'He cometh,
And no bee hummeth.'

> 'O children, come in from your soldier-play
> In the black bean tents! The night is falling;
> Owls with their shuddering cry are calling;
> A dog howls, lonely, far away.'

> His son comes in like a ghost through the door.
> He'll be ready, maybe, for the next big war.

> O world, come in from the leasowes grey
> And cold, where swaths of men are lying,
> And horror to shuddering horror crying!
> Come home
> To the wisdom of those that till the loam,
> And give man time for his working-day!

Then the white-blossomed ash will sing – 'He cometh,
For whom the loving-cup is poured, the wild bee hummeth.'

M. Winifred Wedgwood

THE V.A.D. SCULLERY-MAID'S SONG

Washing up the dishes;
    Washing up the plates;
Washing up the greasy tins,
    That everybody hates.

Scouring out the buckets;
    Cleaning down the stoves.
Guess I'm going to 'stick it',
    Though my fancy roves.

Washing 'for duration',
    That's what I will do;
As I've got no head-piece
    For the cooking too.

Others are much smarter;
    More clever, too, than I.
Still I go on 'charing';
    Singing cheerfully –

'Washing up the dishes;
    Washing up the plates;
Washing up the greasy tins,
    Which everybody hates.'

CHRISTMAS, 1916
Thoughts in a V.A.D. Hospital Kitchen

There's no Xmas leave for us scullions,
    We've got to keep on with the grind:
Just cooking for Britain's heroes.
    But, bless you! we don't really mind.

We've scores and scores of potatoes,
    And cabbages also to do;
And onions, and turnips, and what not,
    That go in the Irish Stew.

124

We're baking, and frying, and boiling,
From morning until night;
But we've got to keep on a bit longer,
Till Victory comes in sight.

Then there's cutting the thin bread and butter,
For the men who are very ill;
But we feel we're well rewarded;
For they've fought old Kaiser Bill.

Yes! we've got to hold on a while longer,
Till we've beaten the Hun to his knees:
And *then* 'Good-bye' to the kitchen;
The treacle, the jam, and the cheese!

THE POET AND THE BUTCHER

Milton, thou shouldest be living at this hour,
England hath need of thee. She is a den
Of sugar cards and meatless days and feasts,
Yclept of all their wonted pageantry.
O organ voice of England, who but thee
Could conjure Sunday joints for coupons vile
And fright the butcher from penurious ways,
Provoked by Rhondda and his baleful crew?
Nature, good cateress, once you called her so,
Means her provisions only for the good,
And therefore, looking at the piece of meat
Reposing doleful on our platter blue,
We know we must be bad, O very bad,
And quite unworthy, Milton, John, of you.
That being so, forgive me if I stop
And ask your leave to let the matter drop.

May, 1918

Lucy Whitmell

CHRIST IN FLANDERS

We had forgotten You, or very nearly –
You did not seem to touch us very nearly –
   Of course we thought about You now and then;
Especially in any time of trouble –
We knew that You were good in time of trouble –
   But we are very ordinary men.

And there were always other things to think of –
There's lots of things a man has got to think of –
   His work, his home, his pleasure, and his wife;
And so we only thought of You on Sunday –
Sometimes, perhaps, not even on a Sunday –
   Because there's always lots to fill one's life.

And, all the while, in street or lane or byway –
In country lane, in city street, or byway –
   You walked among us, and we did not see.
Your Feet were bleeding as You walked our pavements –

How *did* we miss Your Footprints on our pavements? –
   Can there be other folk as blind as we?

Now we remember; over here in Flanders –
(It isn't strange to think of You in Flanders) –
   This hideous warfare seems to make things clear.
We never thought about You much in England –
But now that we are far away from England –
   We have no doubts, we know that You are here.

You helped us pass the jest along the trenches –
Where, in cold blood, we waited in the trenches –
   You touched its ribaldry and made it fine.
You stood beside us in our pain and weakness –
We're glad to think You understand our weakness –
   Somehow it seems to help us not to whine.

We think about You kneeling in the Garden –
Ah! God! the agony of that dread Garden –
   We know You prayed for us upon the Cross.

Lucy Whitmell

If anything could make us glad to bear it –
'Twould be the knowledge that You willed to bear it –
    Pain – death – the uttermost of human loss.

Though we forgot You – You will not forget us –
We feel so sure that You will not forget us –
    But stay with us until this dream is past.
And so we ask for courage, strength, and pardon –
Especially, I think, we ask for pardon –
    And that You'll stand beside us to the last.

GERVAIS

(Killed at the Dardanelles)

Bees hummed and rooks called hoarsely outside the quiet room
Where by an open window Gervais, the restless boy,
Fretting the while for cricket, read of Patroclos' doom
And flower of youth a-dying by far-off windy Troy.

Do the old tales, half-remembered, come back to haunt him now
Who leaving his glad school-days and putting boyhood by
Joined England's bitter Iliad? Greek beauty on the brow
That frowns with dying wonder up to Hissarlik's sky!

Marjorie Wilson

TO TONY (AGED 3)
(In Memory T.P.C.W.)

Gemmed with white daisies was the great green world
Your restless feet have pressed this long day through –
Come now and let me whisper to your dreams
A little song grown from my love for you.

There was a man once loved green fields like you,
He drew his knowledge from the wild birds' songs;
And he had praise for every beauteous thing,
And he had pity for all piteous wrongs. . . .

A lover of earth's forests – of her hills,
And brother to her sunlight – to her rain –
Man, with a boy's fresh wonder. He was great
With greatness all too simple to explain.

He was a dreamer and a poet, and brave
To face and hold what he alone found true.
He was a comrade of the old – a friend
To every little laughing child like you.

.   .   .

And when across the peaceful English land,
Unhurt by war, the light is growing dim,
And you remember by your shadowed bed
All those – the brave – you must remember him.

And know it was for you who bear his name
And such as you that all his joy he gave –
His love of quiet fields, his youth, his life,
To win that heritage of peace you have.

❋ *Biographical Notes*

Biographical information has been supplied where possible, though in some cases it is incomplete.

LILIAN M. ANDERSON. Born in Norfolk. Educated at St Mary's Priory, Torquay. Married a Mr Robertson and lived in Axminster, Devon.

MAUD ANNA BELL. Actively promoted the Serbian Relief Fund and other war charities.

VERA BRITTAIN (1896–1970). Author, journalist and lecturer. Born in Newcastle-under-Lyme but spent her childhood in Macclesfield and Buxton. Educated at St Monica's, Kingswood, and Somerville College, Oxford, which she entered as an Exhibitioner in 1914. Abandoned Oxford temporarily to serve as a Voluntary Aid Detachment nurse during the war. Her experiences are recorded in *Testament of Youth*, first published in 1933 and a classic of its kind. At the end of the war, with all those closest to her dead, she returned to Oxford, where she met Winifred Holtby: this friendship continued and sustained her until the latter's untimely death in 1935. Vera Brittain wrote 29 books in all. Married George E. G. Catlin, who was Professor of Politics at Cornell University. Their daughter is the politician Shirley Williams.

MAY WEDDERBURN CANNAN (1893–1973). Poet and novelist. Born in Oxford and educated at Wychwood School. Served in the Voluntary Aid Detachment and in the Intelligence Service during the war. Was engaged to Sir Arthur Quiller-Couch's son Bevil, who died of influenza shortly after the Armistice. Worked for the Oxford University Press in Oxford for some years and was Assistant Librarian at the Athenaeum Club, London. Married Brigadier P. J. Slater.

ISABEL CONSTANCE CLARKE. Born in Plymouth and educated privately. Novelist, poet and biographer, writer of studies of Elizabeth Barrett Browning, Maria Edgeworth and the Brontës.

DAME MARGARET POSTGATE COLE (1893–1980). Born in Cambridge, a professor's daughter. Educated at Roedean and Girton, she was for a short time classics mistress at St Paul's Girls' School before taking up political work in the Fabian Research Department in 1917. Married G. D. H. Cole, socialist writer, economist, labour historian and author. She wrote several books, some in collaboration with her husband – including many detective novels. She was Honorary

131

Secretary of the Fabian Society from 1939, later becoming its President until her death, and also Chairman of the Further Education Committee of London County Council in 1950, becoming an alderman in 1952.

ALICE CORBIN (b. 1881). American. Born in St Louis. Was Associate Editor of the American publication *Poetry* from 1912 to 1916. Married a Mr Henderson and lived in Santa Fé, New Mexico.

NANCY CUNARD (1896–1965). Daughter of Sir Bache and Lady Cunard. After a disastrous marriage she settled in the Paris of the twenties and thirties in high café society and the world of jazz and Cubism. She was photographed by Cecil Beaton, painted by Kokoschka and Wyndham Lewis, and was re-created in novels by Ernest Hemingway and Aldous Huxley. At her home in Normandy she founded the Hours Press, issuing Samuel Beckett's first book and publishing the poems of Ezra Pound, Robert Graves and Richard Aldington. She compiled a negro anthology and celebrated its publication by joining the hunger marchers on the Great North Road in 1934. During the Spanish Civil War she went to Spain as correspondent for the *Manchester Guardian*. In the Second World War she worked for the Free French in London.

ELIZABETH DARYUSH (1887–1976). Born in London, daughter of Robert Bridges, the Poet Laureate. Educated by private tuition. She disowned her first three books of poems published in 1911, 1916 and 1921. Like her father she experimented with syllabics, although she still wrote in more orthodox metres. Her work has been compared with that of Thomas Hardy – 'Hardyesque'. She married Ali Akbar Daryush in 1923 and lived for several years in Persia.

EVA DOBELL (1867–1963). Daughter of Clarence Dobell, the Cheltenham wine merchant and local historian, and niece of the poet Sydney Dobell. Deeply distressed by the suffering and loss of life in the war, she volunteered as a nurse, and also took part in the morale-boosting work of corresponding with prisoners of war. Most of her life was spent in the Cotswolds, but she travelled extensively in Europe and north Africa. She helped and encouraged young poets, and campaigned in print for the protection of wildlife and the countryside.

HELEN PARRY EDEN (b. 1885). Born in London, lived in Enstone, Oxford and Woodstock. Educated at Roedean, Manchester

University and King's College Art School. Contributed verse to *Punch, Pall Mall Magazine, The Catholic Messenger* and other journals. Was a Tertiary of the Servite Order.

GABRIELLE ELLIOT. American. Wrote for war organisations such as the American Fund for French Wounded, the Nursing Committee of the Council of National Defense, etc.

ELEANOR FARJEON (1881–1965). Born in London. Educated privately. She wrote fantasies and children's stories, and was one of those rare authors whose books find a devoted audience among both children and grown-ups. There is a Farjeon award for outstanding work in children's literature. She lived in Sussex and was a friend of the poet Edward Thomas and his wife Helen. She became a Roman Catholic in 1951.

S. GERTRUDE FORD. Worked for the 'women's cause' and appeared to be an ardent feminist. Contributed to *Poetry, Poetry Review* and other periodicals. Wrote *Lessons in Verse-craft* published in London by C. W. Daniel, and edited thirty of the 'Little Books of Georgian Verse' for Erskine Macdonald.

CICELY HAMILTON (1872–1952). Born in London. Educated at private schools in England and Germany. She was a familiar figure on Suffragette platforms. During the war she served in a British women's hospital in France. Worked as a journalist and actress, and was also a playwright. Wrote *The Old Vic* (1926) in collaboration with Lilian Baylis, and *Marriage as a Trade*. Won the Femina Vie Heureuse prize for her short novel *William – an Englishman*. She was awarded a Civil List pension in 1938.

HELEN HAMILTON. Schoolteacher. Enjoyed rock-climbing and published *Mountain Madness* (1922) about her climbing experiences in the Alps.

ADA MAY HARRISON. Student at Newnham College, Cambridge, during the war.

AGNES GROZIER HERBERTSON. Born in Oslo. Educated privately. A novelist, short-story writer and journalist, she lived in Liskeard, Cornwall. Published *Cottons and Cookery: A Comedy for Girls* (Samuel French, 1926).

TERESA HOOLEY (1888–1973). Born at Risley Lodge, Derbyshire. Educated by private governess, then at Howard College, Bedford.

ANNA GORDON KEOWN (1899–1957). Born in London. Educated at Cheltenham Ladies' College and in Dresden and Ireland. Married Philip Gosse. A novelist and poet; the foreword to her *Collected Poems* (Caravel Press, 1953) was written by Siegfried Sassoon.

MARGERY LAWRENCE (d. 1969). Born in Wolverhampton. Novelist, journalist and short-story writer. Married Arthur E. Towle. Lived in Bryanston Place, Bloomsbury. A friend of Shane Leslie and Humbert Wolfe, she was a Bohemian and had an enormous zest for life. She could sing, play and dance, and she painted particularly well.

WINIFRED M. LETTS (1882–1971). Born in Ireland. Educated in Bromley. Served as Voluntary Aid Detachment nurse in 1915 at Manchester Base Hospital. Later joined the Almeric Paget Military Massage Corps, working at Command Depot Camps in Manchester and Alnwick. Married W. H. Foster Verschoyle. Lived in Dublin in the 1930s, and in Faversham, Kent, in the 1940s.

AMY LOWELL (1874–1925). American. Born in Brookline, Massachusetts, into the illustrious and wealthy New England family of Lowells. One of her brothers became President of Harvard, another was Percival Lowell the astronomer. She met Ezra Pound in England in 1913 and sought to influence the Imagist movement. Her quest for a hard-edged, unsentimental American verse was dubbed 'Amygism'. The posthumous edition of her *What's O'Clock* was awarded the Pulitzer Prize in 1925.

DAME ROSE MACAULAY (1889–1958). Born in Cambridge, daughter of G. C. Macaulay, a classical scholar and lecturer in the University. Went to school and college in Oxford, but spent most of her childhood in Italy. A prominent novelist, essayist and poet, she won several major literary prizes, including the Femina Vie Heureuse and the James Tait Black Memorial Prize. Clever and critical, she belonged to the Bloomsbury Group. She was renowned for her enormous vigour and zest for life, which she retained even in old age.

FLORENCE RIPLEY MASTIN (b. 1896). American. Educated at Barnard College, Columbia University. Taught English and creative poetry at Erasmus Hall High School, Brooklyn, New York. A member of the Poetry Society of America and winner of poetry awards. Contributor to *The New York Times,* the *Saturday Review* and other periodicals.

CHARLOTTE MEW (1869–1928). Born in Bloomsbury, daughter of an architect. Educated at the Lucy Harrison School for Girls, Gower Street. Overwhelmed by ill-health, family deaths and poverty, she had a poor opinion of herself and her writing. Her output was small but extraordinary – so much so that she was awarded a Civil List pension on the recommendation of Thomas Hardy, John Masefield and Walter de la Mare. She was a petite, eccentric-looking woman, appearing in mannish clothes at Harold Monro's Poetry Bookshop where poets regularly met. She finally committed suicide.

ALICE MEYNELL (1847–1922). Born in Barnes but spent most of her childhood in Italy. Wife of Wilfred Meynell, the author and journalist, and mother of Everard, Francis and Viola. A poet and essayist, she was converted to Roman Catholicism in 1872 and carried her religious beliefs into her writing. While still a girl, her poems had been warmly praised by established writers. Her output of verse and prose was small but always fine in style and content. She and her husband were on intimate terms in their hospitable home with the great literary figures of the time – Browning, Tennyson, Ruskin, Rossetti, Patmore, Meredith and George Eliot.

RUTH COMFORT MITCHELL (1882–1953). American. Born in San Francisco. Married William Sanborn Young.

HARRIET MONROE (1861–1936). American. Born in Chicago. Educated at the Academy of the Visitation, Georgetown. She lectured on poetry and did some newspaper work, chiefly in literary criticism. Founder of *Poetry*, the first American periodical devoted exclusively to verse, and was its editor from 1912 to 1936.

EDITH NESBIT (1858–1924). Born in London. Educated at a French convent. Spent her early youth in the country at Holstead Hall, Kent. She began her literary career by writing poetry but is best remembered for her children's stories. Married Hubert Bland in 1880. She took a keen interest in socialism, and in 1883 was one of the founders of the 'Fellowship of New Life' out of which, in 1884, sprang the Fabian Society. She was a woman of striking appearance and great personal charm.

HON. ELEANOUR NORTON (b. 1881). Lived in London.

CAROLA OMAN (1897–1978). Born in Oxford, daughter of the historian Sir Charles Oman. Educated at Wychwood School, Oxford. Served as a nurse with the British Red Cross Society on the Western Front from 1916 to 1919. Married Sir Gerald Lenanton. A versatile writer of novels and historical biography, she was awarded the *Sunday Times* annual British literature prize for *Nelson* (1948) and the James Tait Black Memorial Prize for *Sir John Moore* (1953). A Trustee of the National Portrait Gallery, she was made Commander, Order of the British Empire in 1957.

MAY O'ROURKE (b. 1898). Born in Ballymena, then lived in Comber, near Belfast. Her father was a Superviser of Inland Revenue in the Civil Service. The family eventually moved to London, then Dorset. Educated by the Sisters of Sainte Marie at Maumbury House. Became secretary to Thomas Hardy in March 1923, when she was twenty-five, and was the friend and confidante of both Hardy and his wife Florence.

JESSIE POPE (d. 1941). Born in Leicester. Educated at Craven House, Leicester, and North London Collegiate School. Contributed some 200 poems and articles to *Punch*. Wrote humorous fiction, verse and articles for leading popular magazines and newspapers. Married Edward Babington Lenton. Lived in Fritton near Great Yarmouth.

DOROTHY UNA RATCLIFFE (1894–1967). Born at Preston Park, Sussex. Educated privately and in Weimar and Paris. Author of many books of verse and prose. Also wrote peasant plays, devoting herself to the dialects of the Yorkshire Dales where she lived following her first marriage. She was Lady Mayoress of Leeds in 1914. A contributor to many North Country newspapers and magazines, she became President of the Yorkshire Dialect Society. A relative by marriage of the 1st Lord Brotherton, she gave his library to Leeds University and added liberal endowments from his large fortune. She married three times.

URSULA ROBERTS (b. 1887). Born in Meerut, India. Educated in Highgate and at London University. A contributor to literary reviews and periodicals, she was a member of the Executive Anglican Group for Ordination of Women. Married the Rev. W. C. Roberts and lived in Woburn Square, W.C.1. Wrote under the name 'Susan Miles'.

LADY MARGARET SACKVILLE (1881–1963). Daughter of the 7th Earl de la Warr. She was mainly a poet, but wrote some books for children. Much of her life was spent in Edinburgh, although she lived in Cheltenham latterly.

LADY AIMEE BYNG SCOTT (d. 1953). Daughter of General C. H. Hall, she married Major-General Sir Arthur Scott in 1894. She published a number of poems and plays, writing under the name 'Alec Holmes'.

MAY SINCLAIR (1865–1946). Born in Rock Ferry, Cheshire. Educated at Cheltenham Ladies' College. Served with the British Red Cross in a Field Ambulance Corps, Belgium. Her first short story was published in 1895 and her first novel in 1896. She also wrote on philosophical idealism. The best of her popular books were experimental in technique and based on the new Freudian psychology. In her time she was considered one of the greatest of the Georgian novelists, but her work met with far greater success in America than in England.

DAME EDITH SITWELL (1887–1964). Born in Scarborough, sister of Osbert and Sacheverell, into an aristocratic family of wealth and culture. She rebelled at an early age against the social role expected from a young English girl of high birth. Recognised as one of the most eminent women poets of her time and admired for the brilliant experimental patterns of sound and imagery in her poems. *Clowns' Houses* (1918) was her first successful volume of poetry. She earned a reputation for eccentricity by habitually dressing in medieval costume. Converted to Roman Catholicism in 1954, the year she was made a D.B.E.

CICILY FOX SMITH (d. 1954). Born in Lymm, Cheshire. Educated at Manchester High School for Girls. She contributed to many journals, her special subject being the history of the sea. Latterly lived in Sutton Scotney, Hampshire.

MARIE CARMICHAEL STOPES (1880–1958). The pioneer advocate of contraception, she was a Suffragette and palaeontologist. In 1904 she became the first female science lecturer at Manchester University. Her famous book, *Married Love,* sold millions of copies throughout the world. With her second husband, Humphrey Verdon Roe, the aircraft manufacturer, she founded the first birth control clinic in north London in 1921, and throughout a turbulent life devoted to sex education became involved in many legal battles. She kept every scrap of paper – a biographer's dream.

MURIEL STUART (d. 1967). Born in London. She wrote poetry from an early age, her first major work appearing in the *English Review* in 1916. She had encouragement from Thomas Hardy, who called her work 'superlatively good'. Two volumes of poetry were published in 1918 and a third in 1922, followed by an American edition in 1926. In a foreword to the American edition Henry Savage wrote: 'Alice Meynell being dead, there is no English poet living today who is Muriel Stuart's peer.' With Mrs C. A. Dawson Scott, she was a founder member of the P.E.N. Club in 1921.

MILLICENT SUTHERLAND (1867–1955). Millicent Gower, Duchess of Sutherland. First daughter of 4th Earl of Rosslyn. Wrote a graphic account of her impressions of the German invasion of Belgium entitled *Six Weeks at the War* published by *The Times* in 1914. Joined the French Red Cross and took the 'Millicent Sutherland Ambulance' to the front with a doctor and eight nurses. Received the French Croix de Guerre and the Belgian Red Cross 1st Class. Held the Queen's canopy at the coronation of George V. Sometime President of the Scottish Home Industries Association and the Potteries and Newcastle Cripples Guild.

SARA TEASDALE (1884–1933). American. Born in St Louis. Her poetry was much influenced by the work of Christina Rossetti. She was courted by Vachel Lindsay but eventually married a St Louis business-man. Her health failed, she took an overdose of sleeping medicine and was found drowned in her bath.

AELFRIDA TILLYARD (b. 1883). Born in Cambridge. Educated in Lausanne and at the University of Florence. Married Constantine Graham and lived in Oxford.

IRIS TREE (1897–1968). Born in London, daughter of Herbert Beerbohm Tree, the famous actor-manager. Her first poems were published when she was sixteen. She studied art at the Slade and became popular with the Bloomsbury Group. She was married twice, first to American photographer Curtis Moffat, then to Count Friedrich Ledebur. A genuine Bohemian, an eccentric and a wit, original in all aspects of her life and character, she shared a secret studio in London with Nancy Cunard. She was photographed by Cecil Beaton and painted by Augustus John.

ALYS FANE TROTTER (1863–1962). English-born, she went to South Africa in the 1890s with her husband, who was employed by the Cape Colonial Government. Attracted by the beauty of old Cape Dutch houses, she wrote and illustrated *Old Cape Colony* (Constable, 1903). On her return to England she wrote poetry, often contributing to *Punch*, the *Cornhill Magazine* and other periodicals.

KATHARINE TYNAN (1861–1931). Born in Clondalkin, Co. Dublin, daughter of a farmer. A Roman Catholic, she was educated at Siena Convent, Drogheda, and began writing at the age of seventeen. During the war she did philanthropic work and some nursing, and had two sons serving in Palestine and France respectively. A poet and prose writer, she was a leading member of the Celtic literary revival and a friend of Yeats, Parnell, the Meynells and the Rossettis.

ALBERTA VICKRIDGE. Born in Bradford and educated at Bradford Girls' Grammar School. Served as a Voluntary Aid Detachment nurse in the war. Her recreations were printing, verse publishing and astronomy. In 1927 she founded the Jongleur Press and became its editor.

MARY WEBB (1881–1927). Born in Leighton, near the Wrekin, Shropshire, daughter of a schoolmaster. Educated in Southport, she began writing verse at the age of ten, afterwards writing fairy tales. Married Henry B. L. Webb in 1912. She published verse and prose in various newspapers and magazines in England and America before moving to London in 1921, reviewing for *The Bookman* and other periodicals. Best known for her novels which are set in the Welsh border country and portray shy heroines in scenes of rustic beauty. Her literary success dated from the occasion when her work was praised by Stanley Baldwin, then Prime Minister. She was awarded the Femina Vie Heureuse Prize for *Precious Bane,* the best English novel of 1924–5. Her novels are brilliantly satirised by Stella Gibbons in *Cold Comfort Farm.*

M. WINIFRED WEDGWOOD. Served with the Devonshire 26th Voluntary Aid Detachment.

CATHERINE DURNING WHETHAM. Lived in Ottery St Mary, Devonshire. Married Cecil Dampier and had six children – five girls and one boy. Wrote *The Upbringing of Daughters* (Longmans, 1917).

LUCY WHITMELL. Her poem 'Christ in Flanders' was originally published in *The Spectator* on 11 September 1915 under the initials 'L.W.'; it was reprinted widely and became one of the most popular and most anthologised poems of the war.

MARGARET ADELAIDE WILSON. American. Born in Erie, Pennsylvania, but lived some time in California.

MARJORIE WILSON. Sister of the war poet Captain T. P. Cameron Wilson. Their father was the Rev. T. Cameron Wilson of Little Eaton, Derby. Her war work included service in the War Relief Office and Voluntary Aid Detachment nursing in Netley.

�֎ *Index of First Lines*